D1759725

Gallery Books
Editor Peter Fallon

AUTUMN SKIES

AUTUMN SKIES

*Writers on poems
by Derek Mahon*

Edited by Peter Fallon

Gallery Books

Autumn Skies
is first published
simultaneously in paperback
and in a clothbound edition
on 23 November 2021.

The Gallery Press
Loughcrew
Oldcastle
County Meath
Ireland

www.gallerypress.com

ISBN 978 1 91133 806 2
ISBN 978 1 91133 807 9

A CIP catalogue record for this book
is available from the British Library.

Contents

AUTUMN SKIES

Preface

'This iceberg cuts its facets from within.' This line from 'The Imaginary Iceberg' by Elizabeth Bishop, a poet much admired by Derek Mahon (see Sara Berkeley's essay, pages 111-112, or Derek's own 'Elizabeth Bishop' in *Washing Up*, 2020) might be as good a description as any of the workings of a Mahon poem as he locates the 'places where a thought might grow' and finds a fitting form for it. In poems such as the immaculate 'Antarctica' or indeed the fabled 'A Disused Shed in Co. Wexford' the poem's idea enacts itself.

The hope of *Autumn Skies* — a phrase first mentioned in 'The Seasons' (*An Autumn Wind*, 2010) — was to present on the occasion of Derek Mahon's eightieth birthday a collection of responses to his poems by writers who have published with The Gallery Press. Alas, it has become a memorial tribute.

The contributors have approached the poems they've chosen in various ways: some offer close readings, some open to experiences prompted by the subject matter of the work. Frank McGuinness, a colleague once, presents biographical detail while recognizing and registering 'the slyest of echoing ironies' of what might be Mahon's best known poem, 'Everything Is Going to Be All Right' (100,000 views on YouTube), a theme Paul Muldoon in a strict, contrarian essay examines further, offering a welcome, corrective contextualization of this poem.

Although Derek Mahon didn't regard 'The Mute Phenomena' as a translation, imitation or adaptation (his translation of 'Vers dorés' appears in *Echo's Grove*, 2013) we are happy to include what might be Seamus Deane's last piece of criticism. It is a pleasant fancy to think that Seamus and Derek might be arguing that toss in their amused and brilliant banter.

The chosen poems include some of his very earliest, short and longer poems in different tones and forms, and some of his very last. A feature of the collection is the responses of a number of younger writers. All this would have pleased Derek. Inevitably, there are references to, even reliances on, earlier versions of certain poems. (This mightn't.)

John Banville and Audrey Molloy, both with origins in our most south-eastern county, address 'A Disused Shed in Co. Wexford', while Bernard O'Donoghue throws light on 'A Garage in Co. Cork'. Medbh McGuckian riffs on resonant, immortal lines from many poems in her consideration of 'Dawn at St Patrick's'. Ailbhe Ní Ghearbhuigh is brought back by 'Global Village' to her time in New York City while Ciaran Berry, now resident in the US, reflects on 'Alien Nation'.

In my own essay I note the coherence of his work. Even in this almost random selection the trajectory of his work (and of his life) may be discerned — from the sense of knowing his place in the poem Caitríona Ní Chléirchín selects to John McAuliffe's choice 'Harbour Lights' which ends with 'to find the right place, find it and live forever' and in 'A Quiet Spot' to 'the perfect work-life balancing act / you've found after so many a fugitive year / of travel'.

Derek Mahon was a master — at once classical and right up to the moment. He is the one to learn from. Frank McGuinness's essay concludes with this apt assessment: 'He is Ireland's Montaigne and his work is for all time.'

— Peter Fallon
Loughcrew
August 2021

Spring in Belfast

Walking among my own this windy morning
in a tide of sunlight between shower and shower,
I resume my old conspiracy with the wet
stone and the unwieldy images of the squinting heart.
Once more, as before, I remember not to forget.

There is a perverse pride in being on the side
of the fallen angels and refusing to get up.
We could *all* be saved by keeping an eye on the hill
at the top of every street, for there it is,
eternally, if irrelevantly, visible —

but yield instead to the humorous formulae,
the spurious mystery in the knowing nod;
or we keep sullen silence in light and shade,
rehearsing our astute salvations under
the cold gaze of a sanctimonious God.

One part of my mind must learn to know its place.
The things that happen in the kitchen houses
and echoing back streets of this desperate city
should engage more than my casual interest,
exact more interest than my casual pity.

Caitríona Ní Chléirchín
Spring in Belfast

At the heart of Derek Mahon's early poem 'Spring in Belfast' is a deep understanding and unconditional love for the 'desperate city' of Belfast. Just as love often accepts tragedy and imperfection, the poet accepts the 'sunlight between shower and shower' and 'sullen silence in light and shade' of his native city. The city becomes the internal location of emotion and memory, fragmented and complex, the city of the mind. As an exile from Belfast there's a feeling of isolation, loneliness and alienation in this poem, even if he is 'walking among [his] own'. Perhaps so, yet, like so many of us, never more alone, never further from home. The real question this poem makes us ask is what is home, where is it and how do we find it or accept it. Is 'the squinting heart' half closed or blinded by 'unwieldy images'? Has some part of the 'wet stone' entered that heart forever? Is there a sense of all the suffering he has tried to forget?

The God of the poet's understanding would seem to be cold and sanctimonious and the poet would prefer to be on the side of the fallen angels 'refusing to get up'. Eternity comes in the shape of the Black Mountain but is somehow irrelevant, although visible. Salvation may have been reached through keeping the mountain in view but instead the people yield to the everyday realities of life and survival in the city. When faced with the still sad music of humanity, the desolation of the human condition, the alternatives are 'humorous formulae', 'the spurious mystery in the knowing nod', 'sullen silence' or 'rehearsing our astute salvations'. The poet is not fooled by any of these and yet there is love for the 'echoing back streets', and a pity beyond all telling.

Is there something unspeakable or just mundane about 'the things that happen in the kitchen houses / and echoing back streets'? Is this ordinary, casual violence and cruelty? There's a strong feeling of a burden of duty and responsibility in the last two lines, even more so for the use of the word 'casual': 'should engage more than my casual interest, / exact more interest than my casual pity'. As it does, in my view.

We see at work here one part of the mind that observes the other, a contradictory, troubled soul that feels the duty of love and care: 'One part of my mind must learn to know its place.' The internalized authoritarian inner father voice is stark, harsh, formulaic, sombre and yet loving. The emphasis is on 'must' and 'should'. The poet sees and knows on many levels, even when he tries not to.

The 'desperate city' is not just Belfast, but the poet and his inner father figure. He holds a stark mirror up to himself and his people. The gaze is intense, unrelenting. Something of the unbearable pain comes across without ever being mentioned explicitly. Northern silence, northern reticence and glimpses of light among the shadows and pain echoes.

Mahon questions *all*.

Carrowdore

at the grave of Louis MacNeice

Your ashes will not stir, even on this high ground,
however the wind tugs, the headstones shake.
This plot is consecrated, for your sake,
to what lies in the future tense. You lie
past tension now, and spring is coming round
igniting flowers on the peninsula.

Your ashes will not fly, however the winds roar
through yew and bramble. Soon the biographies
and buried poems will begin to appear,
but we pause here to remember the lost life.
Maguire proposes a blackbird in low relief
over the grave, and a phrase from Euripides.

Which suits you down to the ground, like this churchyard
with its play of shadow, its humane perspective.
Locked in the winter's fist, these hills are hard
as nails, yet soft and feminine in their turn
when fingers open and the hedges burn.
This, you implied, is how we ought to live —

the ironical, loving crush of roses against snow,
each fragile, solving ambiguity. So
from the pneumonia of the ditch, from the ague
of the blind poet and the bombed town you bring
the all-clear to the empty holes of spring,
rinsing the choked mud, keeping the colours new.

Rosita Boland
Carrowdore

As a student I read my way through Louis MacNeice's *Collected Poems* as if it were a novel. Poem by poem. Page by page. I marked phrases that delighted me. I framed with crayon the poems that spoke to me the most. There were so many I loved, with their musicality and energy and vivid images, but none more so than 'Snow'.

It's that juxtapostion of the summer roses and the winter snow, the lit fire and the segmented tangerine, the drama and high octane beauty of it all. Only twelve lines long, the poem is a swirl of snowstorm, flower petals, flames and a kind of transcendent conclusion. It's a glassy snowglobe of a poem: every time I reread and upend it, it remakes itself both so endlessly, and so beautifully.

To me 'Snow' is a poem at the matrix of Louis MacNeice's work. It encapsulates the essence of his vision, of his sensibility, of what he was trying to achieve as a poet. Which is why it is the perfect poem to pulse through Derek Mahon's masterful elegy, 'Carrowdore'.

'Carrowdore' celebrates MacNeice the person, and his singularity, with the same musicality of a MacNeice poem. But the rest is all Derek Mahon. We are outside, out in the churchyard of a village on the Ards Peninsula in Northern Ireland, out in the wild wind, where trees are flexing and everything is in motion, except the ashes of the dead poet, interred beneath the yews and brambles.

MacNeice's 'ashes will not stir'. They 'will not fly'. He is gone, and even the remains of his mortal self are anchored now to the earth, and not the sky. His as-yet-unpublished poems will surface, however, as will the inevitable analyses of his life and work, in the form of biographies, essays, other attempts at eulogies, though time has revealed that none has surpassed Mahon's one.

And yet there is movement everywhere. Spring with its

heat, creating the fireworks of flowers to burst through the winter clay. The greening hedges. The perpetual future tense. Life is fierce and vigorous, and should be lived with the vigour and ferocity that MacNeice signalled and celebrated. 'This, you implied, is how we ought to live.'

And we are back again into the snowglobe, and the 'ironical, loving crush of roses against snow, / each fragile, solving ambiguity'. Back into the marvel of a world where the opportunity to marvel is inexhaustible. Where a tangerine is portioned and everything is both itself and something else: a fruit sealed in an orange skin is also a collection of segments, studded with pips, and potential for renewal. The flexibility of our possibilities, and the 'drunkenness of things being various'.

Just as there is more than glass between the snow and the huge pink roses, there is more that is welling up in the empty holes of Mahon's Carrowdore spring, the more that will rinse away so much more than mud; a line that keeps on and on resonating.

Beyond Howth Head

for Jeremy Lewis

The wind that blows these words to you
bangs nightly off the black-and-blue
Atlantic, hammering in its haste
dark doors of the declining west
whose rock-built houses year by year
collapse, whose children disappear
(no homespun cottage industries'
embroidered cloths will patch up these

lost townlands on the crumbling shores
of Europe); shivers the dim stars
in rainwater, and spins a single
garage sign behind the shingle.
Fresh from Long Island or Cape Cod
night music finds the lightning rod
of young girls coming from a dance
(you thumbs a lift and takes your chance)

and shakes the radio sets that play
from Carraroe to Dublin Bay
where, bored to tears by Telefís,
vox populi vox Dei, we reach
with twinkling importunity
for good news on the BBC,
our heliotropic Birnam Wood
reflecting an old gratitude.

What can the elders say to this?
The young must kiss and then must kiss
and so by this declension fall
to scrawl the writing on the wall.
A little learning in a parked
Volkswagen torches down the dark

and soon disperses tired belief
with an empiric *joie de vivre*.

The pros outweigh the cons that glow
from Beckett's bleak *reductio* —
and who would trade self-knowledge for
a prelapsarian metaphor,
love-play of the ironic conscience
for a prescriptive innocence?
'Lewde libertie', whose midnight work
disturbed the peace of Co. Cork

and fired Kilcolman's windows when
the Ulster chieftains looked to Spain,
come and inspire us once again!
But take a form that sheds for love
that prim conventual disdain
the world beyond knows nothing of;
and flash, an *aisling*, through the dawn
where Yeats's hill-men still break stone.

I woke this morning (March) to hear
church bells of Monkstown through the roar
of waves around the Seapoint tower
and thought of the lost swans of Lir
when Cormac rang the Christian bell
to crack the fourth-dimensional
world picture of a vanished aeon,
making them human once again.

It calls as oddly through the wild
eviscerations of the troubled
waters between us and North Wales
where Lycid's ghost for ever sails
(unbosomings of seaweed, wrack,

industrial bile, a boot from Blackpool,
contraceptives deftly tied
with best regards from Merseyside)

and tinkles with as blithe a sense
of man's cosmic significance
who wrote his world from broken stone,
installed his word-God on the throne
and placed, in Co. Clare, a sign:
'Stop here and see the sun go down.'
Meanwhile, for a word's sake, the plastic
bombs go off around Belfast;

from the unquiet Cyclades
a Greek poet consults the skies
where sleepless, cold, computed stars
in random sequence light the bars;
and everywhere the ground is thick
with the dead sparrows rhetoric
demands as fictive sacrifice
to prove its substance in our eyes.

Roaring, its ten-lane highways pitch
their naked bodies in the ditch
where once Molloy, uncycled, heard
thin cries of a surviving bird;
and Washington, its grisly aim
to render the whole earth the same,
sends the B-52s to make it
safe for Chase and the stock market.

Spring lights the country; from a thousand
dusty corners, house by house,
from under beds and vacuum cleaners,
empty Calor Gas containers,

bread bins, car seats, crates of stout,
the first flies cry to be let out,
to cruise a kitchen, find a door
and die clean in the open air

whose smokeless clarity distils
a chisel's echo in the hills
as if some Noah, weather-wise,
could read a deluge in clear skies.
But nothing ruffles the wind's breath —
this peace is the great peace of death
or *l'outre-tombe*; make no noise,
the foxes have quit Clonmacnoise.

I too, uncycled, might exchange,
since 'we are changed by what we change',
my forkful of the general mess
for hazelnuts and watercress
like one of those old hermits who,
less virtuous than some, withdrew
from the world circles people make
to a small island in a lake.

Chomēi at Tōyama, his blanket
hemp, his character a rank
not-to-be-trusted river mist,
events in Kyōto all grist
to the mill of a harsh irony,
since we are seen by what we see;
Thoreau like ice among the trees
and Spenser, 'farre from enimyes',

might serve as models for a while
but to return in greater style.
Centripetal, the hot world draws

its children in with loving paws
from rock and heather, rain and sleet
with only Calor Gas for heat
and spins them at the centre where
they have no time to know despair.

The light that left you streaks the walls
of Georgian houses, pubs, cathedrals,
coasters moored below Butt Bridge
and old men at the water's edge
where Anna Livia, breathing free,
weeps silently into the sea,
her tiny sorrows mingling with
the wandering waters of the earth.

And here I close; for look, across
dark waves where bell-buoys dimly toss,
the Baily winks beyond Howth Head
and sleep calls from the silent bed;
while the moon drags her kindred stones
among the rocks and the strict bones
of the drowned, and I put out the light
on shadows of the encroaching night.

Gerald Dawe
Beyond Howth Head

As is the way with Derek Mahon's poetry you need to have your wits about you because he had a penchant for revising, much to the consternation of his devoted fans, which includes the present writer. I first came across 'Beyond Howth Head' as the capstone to Derek's *Lives* published by Oxford University Press in 1972. An earlier version had appeared as a Dolmen Press pamphlet in 1970 but that had not penetrated deepest North Belfast or, so far as I recall, the couple of good bookshops downtown that 'carried' poetry.

The long poem in twenty-three Marvellian stanzas would be tinkered with and by the time of The Gallery Press's magisterial *New Collected Poems* (2011), the 1960s' vibe was tuned down a touch here and there as Mahon shaved off five stanzas and flushed out some time-specific references in other places. Nevertheless, the tone and pace of the *Lives* version stays with me like a favourite record track.

From its opening salutation as a verse letter to his friend Jeremy Lewis ('The wind that blows these words to you / bangs nightly off the black-and-blue / Atlantic') to — in its original version — *Ginger Man*-like conclusion:

> *and here I close my* Dover Beach
> *scenario, for look! the watch-*
> *ful Baily winks beyond Howth Head,*
> *my* cailín bán *lies snug in bed . . .*

the wonderful meditative tidal pulses of the entire poem sweep the reader into a kind of dreamlike state in which the poet registers a current life, somewhat in stasis:

> *The light that left you streaks the walls*
> *of Georgian houses, pubs, cathedrals,*

coasters moored below Butt Bridge
and old men at the water's edge . . .

'Beyond Howth Head' is also very much a love poem to Dublin and Ireland. Mahon's imagination roams to the west coast, to the south (where of course he would eventually settle a quarter of a century after publishing the poem) and identifies with his predecessors from Spenser to Yeats and Beckett. The literary references are worth a quiz all to themselves.

But what impresses is the merging of all this intelligence with the personal moment and the political 'global' state of things. Mahon, in his late twenties, was already marrying the light touch of a Robert Graves with the darker tones of repression as it struck deep into European nation states — such as Greece — and the appalling imperialism of the US disaster in Vietnam.

How was the poet, never mind the 'Irish' poet, to connect with all these gathering forces without abdicating the crucial independence of his/her playful engagement with artistic form?

Written all over 'Beyond Howth Head' or, should I say, 'inscribed' within it, from Irish myth to present-day readings — again, the original version namechecks Norman Mailer's *Armies of the Night* — there is an abiding sense of the poet as an acknowledging yet private figure such as Thoreau or the Basil Bunting inflected 'Chomēi at Tōyama'; a first outing for that enduring presence in Mahon's poetry of the solitude out of which great poetry is produced, such as his own, 'where Lycid's ghost for ever sails'.

Afterlives

for James Simmons

1

I wake in a dark flat
to the soft roar of the world.
Pigeons neck on the white
roofs as I draw the curtains
and look out over London
rain-fresh in the morning light.

This is our element, the bright
reason on which we rely
for the long-term solutions.
The orators yap, and guns
go off in a back street;
but the faith doesn't die

that in our time these things
will amaze the literate children
in their non-sectarian schools
and the dark places be
ablaze with love and poetry
when the power of good prevails.

What middle-class shits we are
to imagine for one second
that our privileged ideals
are divine wisdom, and the dim
forms that kneel at noon
in the city not ourselves.

2

I am going home by sea
for the first time in years.
Somebody thumbs a guitar
on the dark deck, while a gull
dreams at the masthead,
the moon-splashed waves exult.

At dawn the ship trembles, turns
in a wide arc to back
shuddering up the grey lough
past lightship and buoy,
slipway and dry dock
where a naked bulb burns;

and I step ashore in a fine rain
to a city so changed
by five years of war
I scarcely recognize
the places I grew up in,
the faces that try to explain.

But the hills are still the same
grey-blue above Belfast.
Perhaps if I'd stayed behind
and lived it bomb by bomb
I might have grown up at last
and learnt what is meant by home.

Annemarie Ní Churreáin
Afterlives

What does it mean to bear witness in poetry? How to pursue the poetic image out of trauma, suffering, exile? The violence of Northern Ireland during The Troubles, and what it might have been to face into that violence, or face away from it, is not an experience I know first-hand. And yet in 'Afterlives' I wake as Mahon wakes 'in a dark flat / to the soft roar of the world' and I am reminded of all the shadowy flats and hide-out rooms, the dens and in-between temporary spaces I have lived in, over twenty years, since I left behind my own home place in northwest Donegal. Who of us cannot identify with that waking? Or with the threshold that, once crossed, reveals the world, or ourselves within it, utterly transformed?

To enter into 'Afterlives' is to enter into a moment that I am compelled to think of as distinctly post-death and pre-grief, a moment of pure out-of-body wonder at the up-close strangeness of the landscape and what appears within it; the pigeons, the orators, the 'faces that try to explain'. Like a ghost, or a ghostly lens, death — at every turn — frames and contains the almost alien nature of life itself, and a ripple of shock, or held breath, or awe, seems to haunt each of the poet's lines. In this suspended reality I find myself reckoning with decisions made, with action and consequence, with questions of personal responsibility. But this poem invites me to consider elegance too, along-side beauty and hope. How can such things be possible in the aftermath of bombs? How can it be right? The poem's poise never fails to disorientate me, and in this disorientation I glimpse, just for a second, not only the invisible threads that bind Mahon to Northern Ireland but the threads that bind me to my home place which I see now being gradually eroded and clinging, despite the odds, to language, tradition, ritual.

'But the faith doesn't die.' Dreams prevail and, word by word, I am drawn into a vast 'shuddering' rebirth. The great mother-force of the ocean carries the ship safely to harbour, among waves of music, space, imagination. That life goes on regardless, that will endures, that language is a form of reconciliation with what can never be fully understood — that, for me, is the pulse and grace of this masterful poem. 'I step ashore in a fine rain' and, washed clean again by that rain, anything can happen. As if by magic I am pulled through a tunnel of time to find myself back in the spot where I started out. In the summer of 1995 I was only a teenager when The Poets' House arrived at the foot of Errigal and a director of the house — the poet James Simmons — handed me a thin, yellow pamphlet titled *Light Music*. It was my first introduction to Derek Mahon. A light came on inside a room I did not know I had.

Leaves

The prisoners of infinite choice
have built their house
in a field below the wood
and are at peace.

It is autumn, and dead leaves
on their way to the river
scratch like birds at the windows
or tick on the road.

Somewhere there is an afterlife
of dead leaves,
a forest filled with an infinite
rustling and sighing.

Somewhere in the heaven
of lost futures
the lives we might have led
have found their own fulfilment.

Vona Groarke
Leaves

Would that every choice would result, not in chaos, strife or disappointment, but in a slant-rhyming 'peace', as happens in the first stanza of 'Leaves'!

Not that it's a reassuring poem, exactly, for all the neatness of its four quatrains and precise, surgical language that still manages to include in its sweep a lyric elegance.

A strange first stanza it is, with its obscure proposal that flits between abstraction and specificity. We can't help but visualize the house in a field below the wood, because that is what concrete detail in a poem begs of us. We might be less clear about who the prisoners of infinite choice might be, or why they should now be at peace. The attempt to resolve that puzzle would have us asking, perhaps, if a rural retreat is always and inevitably the best answer to the kind of consumerist frenzy (the 'infinite choice'?) that some might say an urban life entails. If we don't agree that it does, or that it is, we might be tempted to stop right there, as the suspicion that the house perhaps houses a podium (and a megaphone?) takes hold.

But that stopping would be a mistake because what happens next is that the poem, standing watchfully outside that house, activates it with dramatic description, bringing it to vivid life. Dead leaves are heard to scratch like birds or tick like clocks (or bombs?). It's a kind of aural image, one that implicates us in listening and seeing, so the sensory response is privileged above the intellectual (or moral) one.

That way of squaring off a philosophical (or dogmatic) position while, at the same time, extending a kind of sensory invitation to the reader, seems to me to be characteristic of the best Derek Mahon poems. Admiring how the language shimmies between instruction and evocation, I greatly value how he trusts his imagery to do the heavy lifting where a lesser poet would resign the poem to rhetoric or cant.

Stanza three, in the original verison, expands the house to a stadium. Stanza four extends it to a heaven. It's risky: if everything, no matter how small, can be converted into something more significant, might the poem, in plying its inflationary metaphors, not also seem to lay claim to the possibility of infinite choice so denigrated in the poem's first line? But no; metaphor's greedy, consumerist tendencies are immediately checked: yes, the leaves inside the stadium are flipped to human presences (sighing), but they're still leaves, rustling, howsoever infinitely.

That half-pivot between the literal and figurative (between fact and speculation?) accommodates a shift into a fourth-stanza register closer to stanza one. We're back to an abstract proposition — 'the heaven / of lost futures' and 'the lives we might have led'. This accordion-like movement between little and large, where neither seems either under- or overdone, is quite extraordinary. That we may recognize it from other Mahon poems ('A Disused Shed in Co. Wexford', for example, where a growth of mushrooms, almost incredibly but certainly magically, speak for history's victimized, and it is not an implausible strain) does not diminish its effect.

Fussier language or ornamental flourish would have ruined it but there's something about the restrained elegance of the phrasing and arrangement here that wins our trust. We don't come out of a Mahon poem such as this and think (as we may do with the authoritative pronouncements of lesser but louder poems), 'Oh yeah?'. Poems with greater designs on us, with an argument requiring a single and particular response (usually agreement), are likely to incur resistance: nobody likes to be herded or manipulated, at least not blatantly.

It's a great charm of a good Mahon poem, to ply opinion without alienating readers who might not agree with it. I don't know that I disagree with 'Leaves', but neither am I sure that I'm entirely of a mind. I'm not even particularly sure what the poem's argument is, beyond its bi-play of somewhat categoric statement and the contrasting sinuousness of its imagery. It's a subtle, wishful argument, quietly offered, and with the kind of strangeness at the heart of it that allows the poem to wriggle out of the most fixed and definitive of its opinions. It's a soft speculation, really, that finishes the poem: who could argue against it? Who could doubt it?

Who would ever want to?

The Mute Phenomena

after Nerval

Your great mistake is to disregard the satire
bandied among the mute phenomena.
Be strong if you must, your brisk hegemony
means fuck-all to the somnolent sunflower
or the extinct volcano. What do you know
of the revolutionary theories advanced
by turnips, or the sex life of cutlery?
Everything is susceptible, Pythagoras said so.

An ordinary common-or-garden brick wall, the kind
for talking to or banging your head on,
resents your politics and bad draughtsmanship.
God is alive and lives under a stone;
already in a lost hubcap is conceived
the ideal society which will replace our own.

Seamus Deane
The Mute Phenomena

This is nowhere near being Derek Mahon's finest poem. In the first place, it is a translation or, more accurately, an imitation/adaptation of 'Vers dorés' (Golden Lines), a sonnet by Gérard de Nerval, from his sequence *Les Chimères,* which Mahon translated in 1982. Ever since Gustave Doré's lithograph displaying Nerval's tragic death in 1855 he has been a cult Romantic hero, André Breton and Proust among his champions. The most thoroughly *maudit* of the *poètes maudits,* an afflicted bunch that has since been backlit as the precursors of a more celebrated posterity, Nerval has been invoked by Mahon as a shadow figure for himself, given to addiction and to a subjectivity so extreme ('le rêve est une seconde vie') that it reversed itself in Nerval's poetry and prose into a submission to the atomic life of the world of material phenomena, the cosmic universe in which human beings, thinking themselves the creators of all, blindly and foolishly exist. Mahon's sardonic rendering of this condition is in great part achieved by the tone of the translation, a tone that is reproduced in all his major poems, crisp, dismissive, addressed to a reader who is instantly incriminated, part of a general indictment — 'Your great mistake', 'your brisk hegemony / means fuck-all', 'resents your politics' — but is then finally admitted to be, along with the poet, one of us, a member of the Mahonian afterworld (*Afterlives* is the title of a 1975 book), where we all fade out together, briefly included only to be ultimately excluded together, *not* members of 'the ideal society which will replace our own'.

Mahon likes ruin, debris; it is a recurrent trope in his poetry. Northern Ireland is its most obvious point of reference. Its polar opposite is vision. But vision has no basic reference in modernity, except as artists provide it, Nerval in this instance. In other Mahon poems, it may be

Beckett, MacNeice, or the many others (Baudelaire, Rilke) in whom we encounter obsession, ennui, anomie, addiction, a sense of catastrophe, especially when these are displayed with all the formal powers that art deploys both to assert and subvert itself. A sonnet is famously structured as a form that releases the collective appeal that underlies the individual impulse. Even in his title — not Nerval's — Mahon plays with the single syllable against the polysyllabic, the idea of the mute versus the prolix, although he reverses the valences of each.

The supposed quotation from Pythagoras in the last line of the octet here — 'Tout est sensible' in Nerval's epigraph and text — is given a characteristic inflection:

> *Everything is susceptible, Pythagoras said so.*

Pythagoras is now a mythic, not an individualized figure. Mahon opens the French 'sensible' into a larger domain with 'susceptible', a word that here not only indicates a frail vulnerability (as *to* feeling, illness, change) but also a tensile strength (it can be *of* different interpretations, variations etc). And that line increases the impetus of the sextet, because the element of denunciation, commination even, now has to veer towards grief, from 'You' to 'our own', so that both the reader and writer must come to share the alienation that began only with the reader. Of course that rhetorical switch actually enhances and effects a change in the whole poem's climate of feeling. It surrenders the chiding for a more elegiac tone, the deeper for being sudden. It is a finale; with its twelve syllables and its even spacing, it works like a French alexandrine, still slightly parodic, but yet a completion.

The poem has that measured asperity, that dryness of wit and that surge of sudden feeling that Derek Mahon made into a compound unique to his work.

A Disused Shed in Co. Wexford

Let them not forget us, the weak souls among the asphodels.
— *Seferis, Mythistorema*

for J. G. Farrell

Even now there are places where a thought might grow —
Peruvian mines, worked out and abandoned
to a slow clock of condensation,
an echo trapped for ever, and a flutter
of wildflowers in the lift-shaft,
Indian compounds where the winds dance
and a door bangs with diminished confidence,
lime crevices behind rippling rain barrels,
dog corners for bone burials;
and in a disused shed in Co. Wexford,

deep in the grounds of a burnt-out hotel,
among the bathtubs and the washbasins
a thousand mushrooms crowd to a keyhole.
This is the one star in their firmament
or frames a star within a star.
What should they do there but desire?
So many days beyond the rhododendrons
with the world revolving in its bowl of cloud,
they have learnt patience and silence
listening to the rooks querulous in the high wood.

They have been waiting for us in a foetor
of vegetable sweat since civil war days,
since the gravel-crunching, interminable departure
of the expropriated mycologist.
He never came back, and light since then
is a keyhole rusting gently after rain.
Spiders have spun, flies dusted to mildew
and once a day, perhaps, they have heard something —

a trickle of masonry, a shout from the blue
or a lorry changing gear at the end of the lane.

There have been deaths, the pale flesh flaking
into the earth that nourished it;
and nightmares, born of these and the grim
dominion of stale air and rank moisture.
Those nearest the door grow strong —
'Elbow room! Elbow room!'
The rest, dim in a twilight of crumbling
utensils and broken pitchers, groaning
for their deliverance, have been so long
expectant that there is left only the posture.

A half century, without visitors, in the dark —
poor preparation for the cracking lock
and creak of hinges; magi, moonmen,
powdery prisoners of the old regime,
web-throated, stalked like triffids, racked by drought
and insomnia, only the ghost of a scream
at the flash-bulb firing squad we wake them with
shows there is life yet in their feverish forms.
Grown beyond nature now, soft food for worms,
they lift frail heads in gravity and good faith.

They're begging us, you see, in their wordless way,
to do something, to speak on their behalf
or at least not to close the door again.
Lost people of Treblinka and Pompeii!
'Save us, save us,' they seem to say,
'let the god not abandon us
who have come so far in darkness and in pain.
We too had our lives to live.
You with your light meter and relaxed itinerary,
let not our naive labours have been in vain!'

John Banville
A Disused Shed in Co. Wexford

A friend, one of our finest poets, tells of the morning back in the early 1970s when the post brought a typewritten draft of what many consider to be Derek Mahon's finest achievement — though Mahon himself would strongly dispute the very notion of singling out a particular poem for particular praise. My friend read 'A Disused Shed in Co. Wexford', read it again, and turned to his wife and announced that he was giving up poetry. Happily, he didn't; but one understands the impulse. Most great works of art take time to establish their greatness, a few come with the seal of immortality already impressed upon them.

Mahon's poem is linked, through its dedication, with another masterpiece contemporaneous with it. He and the novelist J G Farrell together stumbled one day on the ruins of a hotel in the Wexford countryside, and out of that fortunate accident came not only Mahon's great poem, but Farrell's novel *Troubles*. Both works deal with the quiet and largely unacknowledged dissolution of lives in the midst of violent upheavals. Farrell's novel is set in an hotel on the way to ruin in the War of Independence, while Mahon's poem was published in 1973, a year after Bloody Sunday in Derry, a pivotal moment in our poor country's latest round of 'Troubles'.

Mahon, that most cosmopolitan of poets, would reject the notion of mere topicality adding weight to a work of art. The truly consummate achievements transcend their time. In fact 'A Disused Shed' deliberately widens the perspective from Ireland's tragedies, past and present, and mourns the humble dead everywhere, especially in its daring cry of grief for the 'Lost people of Treblinka and Pompeii!'; daring, in that the victims of the Treblinka concentration camp were the victims of human wickedness, while the destruction of Pompeii was a 'natural' disaster. It may matter to history how the dead died, but does it to the dead?

Mahon's threnody gains in effectiveness from the restraint of its tone. The poet speaks in accents apt to the 'expropriated mycologist' whose long-ago departure left a shedful of mushrooms to jostle in darkness and in 'a foetor / of vegetable sweat since civil war days'. Match this with the poem's companion piece, 'A Garage in Co. Cork', which entertains, delightfully, the fancy of a passing god having immortalized the garage's owners, 'changing to petrol pumps, that they be spared / for ever there, an old man and his wife'. Some die, some live long, in the realm of poetry.

Mahon's own, recent death lends, whatever he might say to the contrary, a renewed poignancy to 'A Disused Shed'. Certain voices when they fall silent leave a ringing reverberation upon the air of afterwards. Indeed, does a great poet's voice ever fall silent? Derek Mahon was wisely sceptical of poetry's claim to outlive the ages of stone and bronze, since all things perish in time. All the same, we frail, passing creatures of the day catch at least a glimpse of 'for ever' in the timeless sublimity of Mahon's supreme poetic masterwork.

Audrey Molloy
A Disused Shed in Co. Wexford

I came late to this poem. My poetry studies at school were limited to the *Soundings* anthology, which included only four Irish poets, and I did not encounter the work of Derek Mahon until 2015. I was just starting to write seriously at the time, and reading widely. I came across it among a slew of beautiful Irish poems selected for RTÉ's *A Poem for Ireland*. I was smitten.

Having grown up in a village in County Wexford (I also worked Saturday nights in the bar of a local nightclub that later burnt down), it was preordained that I was going to fall hard for this poem. Many a bored weekend I spent as a child poking around the guts of abandoned forges and machinery sheds, wary of rust and broken glass. I'd roamed these burnt-out grounds, brought to life so vividly in 'among the bathtubs and the washbasins'.

But it's the following strange and unexpected line, 'a thousand mushrooms crowd to a keyhole', that electrifies me. Where did that metaphor come from? I puzzled over that question for years before a theory emerged: the best metaphors are sometimes born of taking an existing idea and running with it. While there would be nothing fresh in saying that someone (or something) abandoned has been 'left to rot', to take rotting to its logical conclusion and there-fore into the realm of fungi — the biological instruments of organic decay — is inspired. To anthropomorphize them ('Elbow room! Elbow room!') is a further quantum leap of the imagination.

This is a tender poem. It doesn't bang any drum. It implicates not only the reader, but the speaker, in joint responsibility to these 'powdery prisoners' through deft use of the first-person plural pronouns *we* and *us* — 'They have been waiting for us in a foetor', or, 'at the flash-bulb firing squad we wake them with'. When the poet does address the reader in 'They're begging us, you see, in their wordless way' it feels as if we are in it together. The poem is, in the words of Leonard Cohen, 'a revelation in the heart, rather than a confrontation, or a call-to-arms, or a defense'.

Who are they, these mushrooms? For me, they stand for all those left to quietly rot — not just in nursing homes, refugee camps, war zones, orphanages or septic tanks; they are sheep and cattle in live-trade exports, dogs in pounds, mammals and birds at the edge of residential creep, all waiting 'in a foeter' for us 'to do something'.

They stand for others too, back through history. The lines 'cracking lock / and creak of hinges' and 'the flash-bulb firing squad we wake them with' recall images put into poetry by John Montague in his poem 'A Welcoming Party' in which prisoners filmed emerging from concentration camps at the end of the war are described —

> *One clamoured mutely of love*
> *From a mouth like a burnt glove;*
> *Others upheld hands bleak as begging bowls*
> *Claiming the small change of our souls.*

Some poems move me every time I read them. I'm grateful I don't have to teach 'A Disused Shed in Co. Wexford', where repeated readings might risk my becoming inured to its effect. It's as impressive as any single poem I've encountered, and could be the one Mahon refers to in his poem 'Heraclitus on Rivers' when he writes —

> *Your best poem, you know the one I mean,*
> *the very language in which the poem*
> *was written, and the idea of language,*
> *all these things will pass away in time.*

I carry this poem in my heart and my head. I regret that I never had the opportunity to meet one of the great poets of our age. Recently, while proofreading my debut collection, I noticed how there are tendrils of Mahon's work, and particularly this poem, threading their way into my own poetry as I'm sure they thread into the work of many others. Like the network of fungal mycelium sent out by a great tree to its neighbouring seedlings, perhaps this is another way in which 'a thought might grow':

they lift frail heads in gravity and good faith.

They're begging us, you see, in their wordless way,
to do something, to speak on their behalf
or at least not to close the door again.

The Chinese Restaurant in Portrush

Before the first visitor comes the spring
softening the sharp air of the coast
in time for the first seasonal 'invasion'.
Today the place is as it might have been,
gentle and almost hospitable. A girl
strides past the Northern Counties Hotel,
light-footed, swinging a book bag,
and the doors that were shut all winter
against the north wind and the sea mist
lie open to the street, where one
by one the gulls go window-shopping
and an old wolfhound dozes in the sun.

While I sit with my paper and prawn chow mein
under a framed photograph of Hong Kong
the proprietor of the Chinese restaurant
stands at the door as if the world were young,
watching the first yacht hoist a sail —
an ideogram on sea cloud — and the light
of heaven upon the hills of Donegal;
and whistles a little tune, dreaming of home.

Frank McGuinness
The Chinese Restaurant in Portrush

Just as there is a house in New Orleans they call The
Rising Sun, so there was in Portrush, County Antrim, a
Chinese restaurant opposite the seaside town's crowning
diadem of fading, imperial grandeur, the Northern
Counties Hotel, a perfect model for the Majestic, the ruin
at the heart of Derek's good friend, J G Farrell's novel,
Troubles, a book that had and has its passionate devotees,
Mahon among them. The Northern Counties, a forlorn
Shangri-La then, served drinks throughout the night for
selected aesthetes, staff and students in Coleraine's New
University of Ulster, allowed entry for their intellect,
beauty, recklessness, and infrequent spending power in
tight times, by the town's more advanced connoisseurs of
the art of alcohol, conducting a symposium where debate
could range from the intricacies of melodic patterns in
Japanese folk songs to the more esoteric meanderings of
the French Symbolists. A gentle giantess of a blonde bar-
maid, her hair in a black bow borrowed from Manet's
serveuse at the Bar of the Folies-Bergère, ruled this clean
establishment serenely but with polite severity well into
the morning, providing a refuge without threat or violence
in a Northern Ireland of the 1970s, a place and time
plagued with terrible threats and afflicted with filthy
violence. While he worked as Writer-in-Residence at NUU,
Derek Mahon on occasion served time there, and who
could blame him? There was not much else to console the
poet in that stark, shivering outpost of learning.

My first academic job was teaching in the School of
English at NUU. From time to time my and Derek's paths
crossed, for we shared a dear friend in the Department, Dr
Bridget O'Toole, a deeply learned, deeply read Cornish
woman. I was in numb awe of him, the writer of 'A
Disused Shed in Co. Wexford', inspired by Farrell's novel,

and Jim Farrell was one of what Bridget would call her gentleman callers. She's even mentioned among a list of guests at a ball in the book, arriving last as always. I thought Derek's poem the equal to anything Yeats conjured sailing to or arriving in Byzantium, the poems marrying sound and image in confounding complexity. Derek's private life then was not easy, far too muddled and in pain beyond my sorting, not willing to comprehend what troubled the man. He made no secret of his antipathy at times to that place, hence his later refrain from 'The Sea in Winter', 'Portrush, Portstewart, Portballintrae, / *un beau pays mal habité*'. His loathing would concentrate on the college canteen's food, or this swill as he denounced it once, loudly scraping it into the nearest bin, in full view of the chef, God forgive the description. It is so apt then that the town's one Chinese restaurant and its prawn chow mein should be commemorated in this troubled, troubling poem from a rough time in Derek's life. He did sit alone there, you could glimpse him reading a book or *The New Statesman* or *The Listener*, magazines to which he contributed, ensconced in that restaurant a few doors down from the rooms he rented on the Main Street. Interruptions were clearly not welcome, for he dined there with his most austere Moderator's gaze on his face, and I never broke into that private reverie, for it was a look challenging all comers to dare irk him. That is why I read the poem with near fearful pleasure.

I admire the poem for the dexterity of Mahon's thinking, because in it disillusionment buries itself everywhere, shattering in its eventual explosion hopes and dreams as insubstantial as those in that monument to dejection, 'Everything Is Going to Be All Right', now championed as a beacon of hope in these darker days, oblivious to its slyest of echoing ironies. Here that staunchly Protestant town, Portrush, is quiet, it is spring, before the yearly beating drums of July and the influx of Orange banners, bands and advancing foot soldiers, marching ever onward.

What might have been 'gentle, almost hospitable' — that 'almost' a perfect Mahon giveaway — soon seems beyond the beyonds of possibility, for nirvana cannot be attained within this settlement, armed as it must be against north winds and sea mists, the shops shut all winter now opening their doors to straying gulls and passing, transient girls, indifferent to the gaze of a middle-aged poet who notes at the same time as they a dozing, old wolfhound who, my memory serves, his Fianna and Finn McCool days long gone, is unable even to raise a bark, let alone start a barney with other curs to enliven this joint.

Restraint prevails at the meal. No meat nor wine occupy the table. The fare is quite penitential, even Romanish in its dietary prohibitions, as close to blasphemy as Mahon teases us here. The fabled mysteries of the East contain their secrets within a frame, the sweep of Hong Kong — a favourite lure for many RUC officers in search of adventures abroad — now reduced to a snapshot. The restaurant owner, if he is not inscrutable, then he is rendered immobile, 'stand[ing] . . . watching' at the door, dreaming of a younger world, a place where yachts sail, but here in Portrush even words can only aspire to be what shape they are denied, ideograms, as the sea clouds darken into a calligraphy typed on a page, heaven lying perhaps across the border, so near, so far in the mountains of a Red China of alien Donegal, a forbidden territory with neither the music of a little tune nor the bask of light allowing access to those who inhabit the restaurant, the town, the province, the state of Ulster itself. The quality of Derek Mahon's resilience now moves me above all else in this Chinese puzzle of a poem. How he must have felt his isolation exploiting that most creative of paradoxes, in exile at home. Any wonder the writers I remember him discussing most fluently were Ovid and Malcolm Lowry, Ovid in his native, all-consuming Rome obsessed with things changing until he too is changed into exile and Lowry the novelist melting the lava of his fiction with the savage indignation of a Swift, who is always somewhere near in Derek Mahon's poetry.

Even as a young teacher I knew Derek Mahon was our strangest poet. Throughout his existence on the earth he found a courage to go on, and go on, and go on, steeped in the conviction of his contradictions, able to continue suffering, continue writing, and continue laughing. He is Ireland's Montaigne, and his work is for all time.

North Wind

I shall never forget the wind
on this benighted coast.
It works itself into the mind
like the high keen of a lost
Lear spirit in agony
condemned for eternity

to wander cliff and cove
without comfort, without love.
It whistles off the stars
and the existential, stark
face of the cosmic dark.
We crouch to roaring fires.

Yet there are mornings when,
even in midwinter, sunlight
flares, and a rare stillness
lies upon roof and garden —
each object eldritch-bright,
the sea scarred but at peace.

Then, from the ship we say
is the lit town where we live
(our whiskey-and-forecast world),
a smaller ship that sheltered
all night in the restless bay
will weigh anchor and leave.

What did they think of us
during their brief sojourn?
A string of lights on the prom
dancing mad in the storm —
who lives in such a place?
And will they ever return?

The shops open at nine
as they have always done,
the wrapped-up bourgeoisie
hardened by wind and sea.
The newspapers are late
but the milk shines in its crate.

Everything swept so clean
by tempest, wind and rain!
Elated, you might believe
that this was the first day —
a false sense of reprieve,
for the climate is here to stay.

So best prepare for the worst
that chaos and old night
can do to us: were we not
raised on such expectations,
our hearts starred with frost
through many generations?

Prospero and his people never
came to these stormy parts;
few do who have the choice.
Yet, blasting the subtler arts,
that weird, plaintive voice
sings now and for ever.

Andrew Jamison
North Wind

My first encounter with the poetry of Derek Mahon was in my first year at university in London, at an excellent lecture on 'A Disused Shed in Co. Wexford', given by an English 'Professor of Irish Literature' who repeatedly mispronounced his surname as 'Mahóne' instead of 'Máhon'. This mispronunciation, however trivial, has come to symbolize for me the ambiguity, and conflicted identity, at the heart of Mahon's poetry.

One of the great writers about the coast, particularly the north coast of Ulster, in 'North Wind' he captures its bleakness and beauty. In his essay 'The Coleraine Triangle' he paints a fairly grim view of the area but does concede at one point that it's 'a sort of Ulster riviera, with Portrush as its Nice'.

The poem opens with the simple, inviting phrase 'I shall never forget the wind / on this benighted coast' with 'benighted' meaning both obscured by darkness and contemptibly ignorant, morally and intellectually. This sense of ambiguity reverberates throughout the poem. The opening's simple yet assertive tone echoes Louis MacNeice's opening to 'Wolves': 'I do not want to be reflective any more', another poem (in a long line of Irish poems) about windy weather, in which he does not want to stress the 'flux' or 'permanence' of the tide, as he attempts to block out 'the wolves of water / Who howl along our coast'. Permanence is exactly what Mahon is exploring in this poem, however, as he writes, darkly, of 'our hearts starred with frost / through many generations' and refers to the howling wind as 'like the high keen . . . condemned for eternity'. The use of 'keen' emphasizes the sense of wailing and lamentation, while the 'starred' gives a sense of the people being distinct yet somehow diseased, perhaps referring to the 'wrapped-up bourgeoisie', the Northern Irish or simply the Irish. Mahon, then, is confronting the wind and everything it symbolizes as opposed to trying to block it out with 'talk and laughter' like MacNeice.

Also comparable to Heaney's 'Storm on the Island', both poems are concerned with the Romantic idea of the sublime. We only need to compare Heaney's 'We are prepared: we build our houses squat' with Mahon's 'best prepare for the worst . . . were we not / raised on such expectations?' Both poems about storms, they become larger metaphors for Northern Ireland. In Mahon's poem, however, the wind seems to be less violent than Heaney's 'tragic chorus' and more persistently nagging as he characterizes it as a 'weird, plaintive voice', which 'sings now and for ever'. This is not Muldoonian 'new weather' but rather old weather 'here to stay'. Mahon's use of 'sings' also hints at beauty or at least enchantment, and leaves us with a finely balanced ambiguity about his relationship with Portrush, the north wind, and indeed Northern Ireland. The sea is 'scarred but at peace', after all.

But we have come to expect such ambiguity from the poet who famously stated 'poetry is the other thing that is the other thing'. Indeed, the coast features so much in his writing that we can view it as a symbol for ambiguity in itself. John Montague (a kindred poetic spirit to Mahon) wrote 'on the edge is best', and 'North Wind' is a poem on the edge, literally and figuratively. Lamentation, lambasting and love poem all at once, it captures the essence of his work.

Courtyards in Delft

— Pieter de Hooch, 1659

for Gordon Woods

Oblique light on the trite, on brick and tile —
immaculate masonry, and everywhere that
water tap, that broom and wooden pail
to keep it so. House-proud, the wives
of artisans pursue their thrifty lives
among scrubbed yards, modest but adequate.
Foliage is sparse, and clings; no breeze
ruffles the trim composure of those trees.

No spinet-playing emblematic of
the harmonies and disharmonies of love,
no lewd fish, no fruit, no wide-eyed bird
about to fly its cage while a virgin
listens to her seducer, mars the chaste
perfection of the thing and the thing made.
Nothing is random, nothing goes to waste.
We miss the dirty dog, the fiery gin.

That girl with her back to us who waits
for her man to come home for his tea
will wait till the paint disintegrates
and ruined dykes admit the esurient sea;
yet this is life too, and the cracked
outhouse door a verifiable fact
as vividly mnemonic as the sunlit
railings that front the houses opposite.

I lived there as a boy and know the coal
glittering in its shed, late-afternoon
lambency informing the deal table,
the ceiling cradled in a radiant spoon.

I must be lying low in a room there,
a strange child with a taste for verse,
while my hard-nosed companions dream of war
on parched veldt and fields of rainswept gorse.

Peter Sirr
Courtyards in Delft

Ever since I first read it in the original Gallery publication
of the same title this poem has kept calling me back,
making me want to sit quietly in front of it the way the
Pieter de Hooch painting must have affected the poet as he
contemplated it in the National Gallery in London. Poems
about paintings aren't always compelling. This is different;
it's not just that it inhabits its scene, it's that it brings
the full weight of the Mahon sensibility to bear on every
aspect. There's the scene itself, of course, the Dutch school
stillness, the sense of nothing yet everything happening,
the extraordinary animation of the inanimate. Mahon deftly
sets the scene in the opening lines, but immediately moving
beyond what is in front of him to a kind of omnipresence,
the force of his *everywhere*: ' . . . everywhere that / water
tap, that broom and wooden pail' servicing all that house-
proud thrift and *huiselijkheid*. And straight away there's
something unexpected: the movement from what is there,
everywhere, to what is not to be found. There's no disturb-
ing breeze, no music, nor any of the juicy consolations of
a more fulsome and decadent art. Yet that list of absences
is itself hypnotically powerful, gorgeously present, a painful
acknowledgement of the limitations as well as the oppor-
tunities of art. And that notion is pursued in the image
of the girl who will wait for her lover 'till the paint dis-
integrates / and ruined dykes admit the esurient sea . . . '
Esurient sea, like the 'lambency' that later informs the
deal table, like the 'vividly mnemonic' sunlit railings, like
the 'coal / glittering in its shed' — the poem's burnished
language snares us, makes us stand before it and look
again. This language is life too, the poem might be saying,
this dimension of perception, this pure art, as well as the
reality it describes, as much as the 'cracked / outhouse door'
or those railings. It's the flourish with which the poem

performs itself . . .

Ultimately the poet inserts himself right into the scene, his own life added to the vivid palate. An earlier version had a very different, future-centred conclusion that seemed to admit the light and peace cancelling effects of colonialism and wars:

> For the pale light of that provincial town
> will spread itself, like ink or oil,
> over the not yet accurate linen
> map of the world which occupies one wall
> and punish nature in the name of God.

That's banished now: now we have the excited apprehension of glittering coal, 'late-afternoon / lambency informing the deal table, / the ceiling cradled in a a radiant spoon'. The violent futures that plot themselves in images of 'fire and sword' (from the earlier version) . . . 'on parched veldt and fields of rainswept gorse' are left to that slightly awkward long last line, as if their ugliness and violence needs to be spelled out to be rejected in favour of the truth of art which is the poem's ultimate offering.

Everything Is Going to Be All Right

How should I not be glad to contemplate
the clouds clearing beyond the dormer window
and a high tide reflected on the ceiling?
There will be dying, there will be dying,
but there is no need to go into that.
The lines flow from the hand unbidden
and the hidden source is the watchful heart;
the sun rises in spite of everything
and the far cities are beautiful and bright.
I lie here in a riot of sunlight
watching the day break and the clouds flying.
Everything is going to be all right.

Paul Muldoon
Everything Is Going to Be All Right

It's hard not to experience a sense of joy and possibility in the face of Bob Marley's great 1977 song, 'Three Little Birds', with its upbeat refrain:

> *Rise up this mornin'*
> *Smiled with the risin' sun*
> *Three little birds*
> *Pitch by my doorstep*
> *Singin' sweet songs*
> *Of melodies pure and true*
> *Sayin', 'This is my message to you-ou-ou'*
> *Singin', 'Don't worry about a thing, worry about a*
>   *thing, oh!*
> *Cause every little thing gonna be all right.'*

It's no accident, therefore, that Bob's grandson, Skip Marley, would revisit the song during the 2020 Covid-19 pandemic. Nor is it any accident that the oft-bruited notion that art is a panacea for pretty much anything that ails us should be raised by Donny Mahoney in the Irish pop culture podcast, *The Rewind*:

> *There's little point in trying to whitewash things: the human race is in a difficult moment. We're trying to cope with something that we don't have a whole lot of experience in coping with. Every culture handles adversity in its own unique way. It's been incredible to realize that in Ireland we have a reservoir of strength to draw from when things get hairy. It's called culture. People pay it lip service, others moan about all the funding it gets. Maybe it's only when things get bad that we as a society can fully*

*appreciate how much we value it and actually need
it to function as a people.*

*Isn't it amazing, for instance, that there exists
in this country a succinct, accessible, lyrical and
poignant poetic expression of the philosophical
mantra 'this too shall pass'? It's called 'Everything
Is Going to Be All Right' by the poet Derek Mahon.
Maybe you've heard it on* Morning Ireland *in the
last week, or at the end of* Six One News *on Friday
evening. It's rare for poems to have 'moments', but
Mahon's work has become wonderfully resonant
at this trying time.*

Much as we understand our yearning for a poem that
will deliver what we might term a 'succour-punch', it
betrays an essential misunderstanding of the function of art
and, in this case, a profound inability to recognize irony.

The idea that art may offer the kind of solace more often
associated with religious belief is one that has been asso-
ciated most recently with Seamus Heaney. It must have
come as a bit of a shock to those who ransacked Heaney's
oeuvre for a solid example of poetic consolation in a time
of crisis that they could come up with only 'If we winter
this one out, we can summer anywhere.' Heaney's line,
which comes from a 1972 interview rather than a poem, is
itself an allusion to the great Tyrone poet, W F Marshall:

*Did ye iver know wee Robert? Well, he's nothin' but a
wart,
A nearbegone oul' divil with a wee black heart,
A crooked crabbit crathur that bees neither well or
sick,
Girnin' in the chimley corner, or goan happin' on a
stick;
Sure ye min' the girl for hirin' that went shoutin'
thro' the fair,*

'I wunthered in wee Robert's, I can summer any-
where.

Just as Heaney is indebted to W F Marshall and a phrase spoken by a servant girl, so Mahon is indebted to Bob Marley and a phrase sung by three little birds. That in itself might be a clue as to how seriously Marley himself might have taken it. In December 1976, for example, Marley had survived an assassination attempt in Jamaica and moved to London. 'Three Little Birds' was recorded in London in early 1977 and appeared in June of that year on the album *Exodus*. There is surely some question as to just how 'pure and true' the sentiments of the birds might be. There's an upbeat element, to be sure, but it's chastened just as surely by the broader context of Marley's life and times.

The circumstances in which Derek Mahon found himself in 1977 were no less complex. On one hand he'd taken up a position as Writer-in-Residence at the University of Ulster in Coleraine, his own exodus being from London back to his home turf. On the other his drinking was seriously getting in the way of his life and work. As someone who visited him while he lived in Portrush, and with whom he spent a night or two on the tiles, I can attest to his state being very far from 'all right', with no sign of improvement in sight.

This is not to speak of the state of the nation. In June 1977 a visit to Belfast by Queen Elizabeth II had sparked off not a metaphorical 'riot of sunlight' but a good old-fashioned riot. A year earlier, in August 1976, Portrush had been targeted by members of the Provisional IRA who planted six bombs in hotels and other businesses in the town. No one was killed on that occasion, and though the number of deaths directly related to the Troubles was well down from the 476 of 1972, there were still 295 fatalities in 1976 and 111 in 1977. Hardly a statistic to inspire the chirpiness associated with 'Everything Is Going to Be

All Right'.

The questionable nature of the assertion is further underlined by Mahon's eventual revision of at least one phrase in the poem. This revision is considerably more profound than, say, the substitution in 'A Disused Shed in Co. Wexford' of 'bone burials' for 'shit burials' — a substitution based on the facts of dog behaviour. In this case the shift from 'the poems flow from the hand unbidden' to 'the *lines* flow from the hand unbidden' suggests that Mahon's poems, including this one, are not quite poems in the sense they might be perfect representations of immutable truths. It's as if the poem were further undercutting its own assurance, focusing on the fragmentary rather than the fulfilled.

Another signal from within the poem is the opening phrase 'How should I not be glad to contemplate', where the iambic hastening is simultaneously hobbled by the hesitancy of the idea, like that door in 'A Disused Shed' that 'bangs with diminished confidence'. In a similar vein the bravado of 'There will be dying, there will be dying, / but there is no need to go into that' is hardly meant to be taken unvarnishedly. The true import of that line is that there *is* a need to go into that but perhaps not just now while the speaker tries to shore up his self-delusion. The repetition of 'clouds' in lines 2 and 11 suggests a kind of absentminded desperation rather than conviction. And, again, the last line may be taken at face value only to the extent that we may take at face value the Wordsworth allusion in the last line of this paragraph from Mahon's 1979 *Magill* piece on 'The Coleraine Triangle':

Think of an isosceles triangle, upside-down, with Coleraine as the apex and the twin seaside resorts of Portstewart and Portrush as the base angles. During term time most of the students reside in the base angles. Last year the writer-in-residence resided in Portstewart; this year he resides in

Portrush, in a pleasant whitewashed house with flaking pilasters at the front door and a magnificent sea view. From the window where I write I look eastwards along the shore to the ruins of Dunluce Castle (once a MacDonnell stronghold) and the Giant's Causeway. Slightly to my right is the Royal Portrush golf course, slightly to my left the Atlantic Ocean, with a scattering of rocky islands called the Skerries between me and Scotland. On a clear day I can see Jura and Islay. Earth has not anything to show more fair.

In conclusion, it will be a great day for poetry when we learn to read a poem on the terms it sets up, not those we presume to bring to it.

The Sea in Winter

for Desmond O'Grady

Desmond, what of the blue nights,
the ultramarines and violets
of your white island in the south,
'far-shining star of dark-blue Earth',
and the boat-lights in the tiny port
where we drank so much retsina?
Up here where the air is thinner,
in a draughty bungalow in Portstewart

beside my 'distant northern sea',
I imagine a moon of Asia Minor
bright on your nightly industry.
Sometimes, rounding the cliff top
at dusk, under the convent wall,
and finding the little town lit up
as if for some island festival,
I pretend not to be here at all;

that the shopfronts along the prom,
whose fluorescence blinds the foam
and shingle, are the dancing lights
of Náousa — those gregarious nights! —
that these frosty pavements are
the pavements of that distant star;
that the cold, glistening sea mist
eclipses Naxos to the east.

But morning scatters down the strand
relics of last night's gale-force wind;
far out, the Atlantic faintly breaks,
seaweed exhales among the rocks
and fretfully the spent winds fan
the cenotaph and the lifeboat mine;

from door to door the Ormo van
delivers, while the stars decline.

Portstewart, Portrush, Portballintrae —
un beau pays mal habité,
policed by rednecks in dark cloth
and roving gangs of tartan youth.
No place for a gentleman like you.
The good, the beautiful and the true
have a tough time of it; and yet
there *is* that Hebridean sunset,

and a strange poetry of decay
charms the condemned hotels by day,
while in the dark hours the rattle
of a cat knocking over a milk-bottle
on a distant doorstep by moonlight
can set you thinking half the night.
The moon of Nineveh and Tyre
shines still on the Harbour Bar.

You too know the delirious sense
of working on the circumference —
the midnight oil, familiar sea,
elusive dawn epiphany,
faith that the trivia doodled here
will bear their fruit sometime, somewhere;
that the long winter months may bring
gifts to the goddess in the spring.

The sea in winter, where she walks,
vents its displeasure on the rocks.
The something rotten in the state
infects the innocent; the spite
mankind has brought to this infernal

backwater destroys the soul;
it sneaks into the daily life,
sunders the husband from the wife.

But let me never forget the weird
facticity of this strange seaboard,
the heroism and cowardice
of living on the edge of space,
or ever again contemptuously
refuse its plight; for history
ignores those who ignore it, not
the ignorant whom it begot.

To start from scratch, to make it new,
forsake the grey skies for the blue,
to find the narrow road to the deep
north the road to Damascus, leap
before we look! The ideal future
shines out of our better nature,
dimly visible from afar:
'The sun is but a morning star.'

One day, the day each one conceives —
the day the Dying Gaul revives,
the day the girl among the trees
strides through our wrecked technologies,
the stones speak out, the rainbow ends,
the wine goes round among the friends,
the lost are found, the parted lovers
lie at peace beneath the covers.

Meanwhile the given life goes on;
there is nothing new under the sun.
The dogs bark and the caravan
glides mildly by; and if the dawn

that wakes us now should also find us
cured of our ancient colour-blindness . . .
I who know nothing go to teach
while a new day crawls up the beach.

John FitzGerald
The Sea in Winter

For a time while I was an undergraduate I took to walking the streets of Cork city during the afternoons. There was little structure to my days, except to walk and read; and I followed no particular direction in either. Occasionally, a niggle of shame at being around the city, idle, in the middle of the afternoon, would pull me in to the Central Library on Grand Parade. I always enjoyed re-entry to the hushed stratosphere of its upper floor reference room, where many of my co-readers, young and old, could be slumped in their chairs, asleep or staring into space. It was here that I discovered *The Sea in Winter* by Derek Mahon. A slim Deerfield/Gallery hardback, wrapped in its chocolate-brown paper jacket, one of three hundred copies signed by the author. A couple of years earlier, while still a second level student, I had travelled into Cork by bus to hear the poet read at the new Triskel Arts Centre on Beasley Street. It was the first poetry reading I had ever attended, and I was spellbound by the ritual of the event, by the reader himself, and by the poems, which included 'The Sea in Winter'.

The book wasn't available to borrow, so I would return regularly to replay that flourishing salutation: 'Desmond, what of the blue nights, / the ultramarines and the violets / of your white island in the south.' I wondered how these writers led such charmed lives. How they attained the lyrical rapture to address one another as they did. Why their world was made so dramatic *and* exotic. I grew to love the poem's complicit sense of ennui, bordering on but never quite reaching desolation 'living on the edge of space'; the memorable turns of phrase and allusive colour, both classical and contemporary; the sense of redemption just out of reach; the agonizing, trapped uncertainty of the writing life; all balanced against the consolation of confident, impeccable poetry. For some reason, possibly because I had read Desmond O'Grady's *The Headgear of the Tribe* around the same time, I imagined the poet's correspondent as not on a sun-bleached Greek island at all, but labouring in the gloom of some 'crepuscular valley' somewhere closer to home, at our 'dark edge of Europe'.

There is no doubt that the revised, cropped version of the poem found in the later *Collected* editions, at around half the length of the original, is a more powerful work. But I still revert now and again to the original, to feel the early disconnected end-rhymes fall into the steadier trot of the signature Mahon couplet, impelling the poem past reverie to self-inquiry, and reflection. The undisputed central concern of the earlier version is the dubious value of 'verse-making'. And, while there is some kind of resolution to this dilemma, it is never a lasting one. Instead, there is the familiar consolation of the ordinary ('Meanwhile the given life goes on') which is made to rhyme delightfully, despite itself. The 'luminous geometry' of the poem is all brought to a point by a cinematic cut to an irresistible shot: 'I who know nothing go to teach / while a new day crawls up the beach.' 'The Sea in Winter' was the perfect tonic for my late-adolescent existentialism; and it has remained a very good reason never to have fully recovered.

A Garage in Co. Cork

Surely you paused at this roadside oasis
in your nomadic youth, and saw the mound
of never-used cement, the curious faces,
the soft-drink ads and the uneven ground
rainbowed with oily puddles, where a snail
had scrawled its pearly, phosphorescent trail.

Like a frontier storefront in an old western
it might have nothing behind it but thin air,
building materials, fruit boxes, scrap iron,
dust-laden shrubs and coils of rusty wire,
a cabbage white fluttering in the sodden
silence of an untended kitchen garden —

nirvana! But the cracked panes reveal a dark
interior echoing with the cries of children.
Here in this quiet corner of Co. Cork
a family ate, slept, and watched the rain
dance clean and cobalt the exhausted grit
so that the mind shrank from the glare of it.

Where did they go? South Boston? Cricklewood?
Somebody somewhere thinks of this as home,
remembering the old pumps where they stood,
antique now, squirting juice into a cream
Lagonda or a dung-caked tractor while
a cloud swam on a cloud-reflecting tile.

Surely a whitewashed suntrap at the back
gave way to hens, wild thyme, and the first few
shadowy yards of an overgrown cart track,
tyres in the branches such as Noah knew —
beyond, a swoop of mountain where you heard,
disconsolate in the haze, a single blackbird.

Left to itself, the functional will cast
a deathbed glow of picturesque abandon.
The intact antiquities of the recent past,
dropped from the retail catalogues, return
to the materials that gave rise to them
and shine with a late sacramental gleam.

A god who spent the night here once rewarded
natural courtesy with eternal life —
changing to petrol pumps, that they be spared
for ever there, an old man and his wife.
The virgin who escaped his dark design
sanctions the townland from her prickly shrine.

We might be anywhere but are in one place only,
one of the milestones of Earth residence
unique in each particular, the thinly
peopled hinterland serenely tense —
not in the hope of a resplendent future
but with a sure sense of its intrinsic nature.

Bernard O'Donoghue
A Garage in Co. Cork

'A Garage in Co. Cork' appeared in the *TLS* on 14 May 1982 and in the OUP volume *The Hunt by Night* later the same year where it appears among a group of ekphrastic poems. The other four poems in the group are based on famous paintings, but the title of this poem does not suggest an artistic source at all. It is based on a postcard of a photograph by Fritz Curzon of Gloucestershire which Mahon says he came across in a London bookshop. Though the poem gives no clue, the postcard shows a derelict filling station with the name 'McGrotty's Garage' over it and with two disused petrol pumps outside it. Mahon says he was angered by the Irish stereotyping by 'Curzon's joke', presumably on the name, though no anger survives into the poem.

In fact not much of the occasion of the poem survives at all. The wayside items that are mentioned at the start are the kind of things that you might well see by an abandoned garage in County Cork (in Union Hall maybe, a village visited by Mahon, just off the main route of scenic West Cork), but they are not in the postcard. The address to the 'you' reader at the start is saying 'you know the kind of thing': coagulated unused cement, soft-drink ads, puddles rainbowed by spilled oil. The details come from the imagination, and the second stanza confirms their imaginary nature: the 'frontier storefront in an old western' might indeed be fronting nothing but 'thin air', a false cinematic front. What is behind it too are the things that typical experience of such buildings would lead you to expect as the imagination opens out to a wider perspective — past the contents of building materials, dusty shrubs and rusty wire, into the kitchen garden. At some point such buildings would have housed a family with cries of children: an imaginary scene so bright that the mind 'shrank from the glare of it'.

So where did they go, those children who grew up long ago in West Cork? Typical emigrants went to London or America and would have recalled with homesickness this world they had left. Another 'Surely' invites us to imagine again what must have been there, through a long perspective extending back to Noah. But the things itemized here are the 'antiquities of the recent past' much favoured by Mahon: not only the scenic Celtic past, but the functional too has an afterlife with its own Wordsworthian 'gleam'. Widening out even further the abandoned petrol pumps are mythologized as Philemon and Baucis of Ovid's story, the old couple who here are rewarded for entertaining Zeus by being metamorphosed into petrol pumps as a strange version of eternal life by the roadside. The Daphne of Ovid's story is metamorphosed into the statue of the Blessèd Virgin in her 'prickly shrine'.

On its first publication the poem's title led to association with the poem that had been seen as Mahon's masterpiece so far, 'A Disused Shed in Co. Wexford' at the end of *The Snow Party* in 1975. The original version of the Garage poem had a penultimate stanza which was cancelled by Mahon in the Gallery *Selected* and *Collected* poems. That stanza began in the cosmopolitan, international world of the 'Disused Shed':

> *We might be anywhere — in the Dordogne,*
> *Iquitos, Bethlehem —*

but that perspective is decisively reduced to the locality of this different poem:

> *We might be anywhere but are in one place only.*

That distinctive one place is West Cork, whose history of abandonment is the theme of this haunting poetic feat of imaginative sympathy.

The Globe in Carolina

The earth spins to my fingertips and
pauses beneath my outstretched hand;
white water seethes against the green
capes where the continents begin.
Warm breezes move the pines and stir
the hot dust of the piedmont where
night glides inland from town to town.
I love to see that sun go down.

It sets in a coniferous haze
beyond Georgia while the anglepoise
rears like a moon to shed its savage
radiance on the desolate page,
on Dvořák sleeves and Audubon
bird prints; an electronic brain
records the concrete music of
our hardware in the heavens above.

From Hatteras to the Blue Ridge
night spreads like ink on the unhedged
tobacco fields and clucking lakes,
bringing the lights on in the rocks
and swamps, the farms and motor courts,
substantial cities, kitsch resorts —
until, to the mild theoptic eye,
America is its own night sky.

Out in the void and staring hard
at the dim stone where we were reared,
great mother, now the gods have gone
we place our faith in you alone,
inverting the procedures which
knelt us to things beyond our reach.

Drop of the ocean, may your salt
astringency redeem our fault.

'Blue marble', if we only knew,
in practice as in theory, true
redemption lies not in the thrust
of action only, but the trust
we place in our peripheral
night garden in the glory hole
of space, a home from home, and what
devotion we can bring to it.

You lie, an ocean to the east,
your limbs composed, your mind at rest,
asleep in a sunrise which will be
your midday when it reaches me;
and what misgivings I might have
about the final value of
our humanism pale before
the mere fact of your being there.

Five miles away a southbound freight
sings its euphoria to the state
and passes on; unfinished work
awaits me in the scented dark.
The halved globe, slowly turning, hugs
its silence, while the lightning bugs
are quiet beneath the open window,
listening to that lonesome whistle blow.

Eiléan Ní Chuilleanáin
The Globe in Carolina

I've loved this poem since I first heard Derek Mahon read-
ing it at an event in Trinity some time in the 1990s. The
immediate effect was electrifying, and my first response
was almost all to the rhythms of the verse. The way the
metre moves smoothly ahead while the voice dawdles and
catches up, like a curious dog on a loose lead, almost keep-
ing pace on an interesting road. The way meaning slows —
or accelerates — not only the speaker's pace but the pace of
the listener. The word that is unexpected but not showily
original demands that we give it attention for a slice of
time which is not just a metronomic tick. And all this kept
under control, without ostentation.

I've already started talking about meaning of course,
and indeed the compelling energy of the speaking voice,
the attention we pay it, cannot be merely a matter of
rhythm. The listening is to what the poet is saying not to
the syllabic dexterity. And yet the deployment of lines and
words, evenly contained, keeps the listener's half-conscious
pleasure purring like an engine. For example:

> *From Hatteras to the Blue Ridge*
> *night spreads like ink on the unhedged*
> *tobacco fields and clucking lakes,*
> *bringing the lights on in the rocks*
> *and swamps, the farms and motor courts . . .*

Words you say quickly, almost-hyphenated 'tobacco fields';
words that singly demand their full emphasis, 'Night
spreads' with its obstructive consonants, and the slight un-
expectedness of 'ink'; the lines that land on a strong or
skid on a light note — well, it's almost a pity to underline
the pleasing variety. Meaning, the subject, makes the arch
through which we glimpse the aural attractions. But I've

been emphasizing the musical tempo because that is also in more than one way the subject of the poem. While the verse moves between skipping and strolling, the movement of the globe, measuring the distance, between the poet in North America and — not a place but — a person who is asleep in another time zone, is majestic and even.

The sense of exile is muted and displaced. In an earlier version the cars on the motorway were 'lost meteorites in search of home'. I regret their disappearance, but other metaphorical flourishes, the colours on the globe, call our notice to the grand scale, 'white water seethes against the green / capes where the continents begin'. The global and the cosmic view however narrow down, as the poem ends, to the individual locations, resuming the dense description of the North Carolina landscape, and saluting the remote sleeping figure. In recognizing the importance of the 'mere fact of your being there', the poem returns to human preoccupations, 'unfinished work' and the sound of a passing freight train.

If the world contracts, the train's reminder of distance, of a humanly comprehensible kind, has always seemed to me to be an echo of the earlier reference to music. The 'Dvořák sleeves' in the second stanza recall one of the earliest cultural adventurers from Europe to America, and the steady rhythm of the train in the New World symphony continues for me to throb underneath the metre of Mahon's poem.

Ovid in Tomis

What coarse god
was the gearbox in the rain
beside the road?

What nereid the unsinkable
Coca-Cola
knocking the icy rocks?

They stare me out
with the chaste gravity
and feral pride

of noble savages
set down
on an alien shore.

It is so long
since my own transformation
into a stone

I often forget
that there was a time
before my name

was mud in the mouths
of the Danube,
a dirty word in Rome.

Imagine Byron banished
to Botany Bay
or Wilde to Dawson City

and you have some idea
how it is for me
on the shores of the Black Sea.

I who once strode
head-high in the forum,
a living legend,

fasten my sheepskin
by greasy waters
in a Scythian wind.

My wife and friends
do what they can
on my behalf;

though from Tiberius,
whom God preserve,
I expect nothing.

But I don't want
to die here
in the back of beyond

among these morose
dice-throwing Getes
and the dust of Thrace.

No doubt in time
to come this huddle of
mud huts will be

a handsome city,
an important port,
a popular resort

with an oil pipeline,
smart terraces
and even a dignified

statue of Ovid
gazing out to sea
from the promenade;

but for the moment
it is merely a place
where I have to be.

Six years now
since my relegation
to this town

by the late Augustus.
The *Halieutica*,
however desultory,

gives me a sense
of purpose,
however factitious;

but I think it's the birds
that please me most,
the cranes and pelicans.

I often sit in the dunes
listening hard
to the uninhibited

virtuosity of a lark
serenading the sun
and meditate upon

the transience
of earthly dominion,
the perfidy of princes.

Mediocrity, they say,
consoles itself
with the reflection

that genius so often
comes to a bad end.
The things adversity

teaches us
about human nature
as the aphorisms strike home!

I know the simple life
would be right for me
if I were a simple man.

I have a real sense
of the dumb spirit
in boulder and tree;

skimming stones, I wince
with vicarious pain
as a slim quoit goes in.

And the six-foot reeds
of the delta,
the pathos there!

Whenever they bend
and sigh in the wind
it is not merely Syrinx

remembering Syrinx
but Syrinx keening
her naked terror

of the certain future,
she and her kind
being bulk-destined

for pulping machines
and the cording
of motor-car tyres.

Pan is dead, and already
I feel an ancient
unity leave the earth,

the bowl avoid my eye
as if ashamed
of my failure to keep faith.

(It knows that I
have exchanged belief
for documentation.)

The Muse is somewhere
else, not here
by this frozen lake —

or, if here, then I am
not poet enough
to make the connection.

Are we truly alone
with our physics and myths,
the stars no more

than glittering dust,
with no one there
to hear our choral odes?

If so, we can start
to ignore the silence
of the infinite spaces

and concentrate instead
on the infinity
under our very noses —

the cry at the heart
of the artichoke,
the gaiety of atoms.

Better to contemplate
the blank page
and leave it blank

than modify
its substance by
so much as a pen-stroke.

Woven of wood nymphs,
it speaks volumes
no one will ever write.

I incline my head
to its candour
and weep for our exile.

Seán Lysaght
Ovid in Tomis

'Ovid in Tomis' appeared in *The Hunt by Night* (1982), Derek Mahon's last individual volume with Oxford University Press. While the poem is now established, in a lightly revised and corrected version, within the corpus of the collected work, I still read it in my worn copy of that Oxford volume. This has my signature on the half-title, dated the following year, when I was living in Geneva. My undergraduate efforts with poetry had gradually been overtaken by a drift into academia ('documentation' overtaking 'belief', to use Ovid's terms), but in 1983, having returned to Switzerland from a holiday at home, I wrote a Mahonesque piece, 'In the Burren', which found favour with the editor of the *Poetry Ireland Review*. I think of that acceptance as the moment when I came back to the craft.

'Ovid in Tomis' still sheds its inspiring light from that uncertain time. The author of *Metamorphoses* had been a fixture in the scholarly apparatus during my time as a student of English at UCD, but the opening of this poem was startlingly contemporary. The abandoned gearbox and hair conditioner (now Coca-Cola) have been reiterated many times in Mahon's later work and in the found objects of photography; at the time they struck me with unprecedented freshness. The displaced, dramatized voice seemed casual and colloquial at first, but it made its way through a delightful sequence of rhymes, not strict enough for formality, yet loose enough to give a feel of private expression.

The Augustan world supplied an easy authority that justified what Wordsworth called 'high argument', with an updated, urbane sense of humour never far away; though here the poet keeps that subversive irony at a distance in order to achieve something very hard to sustain in our era:

a poem of ambitious reach without portentousness. Here are lofty pronouncements worthy of early Yeats, such as that 'Pan is dead' and 'The Muse is somewhere / else', alongside the modern self-deprecation of a Prufrock: 'or, if here, then I am / not poet enough / to make the connection'.

I was drawn to Ovid's state of exile as a badge of authenticity, having been nursed in the literature of exile and won over by George Steiner's book *Extraterritorial*, where exile was touted as the very condition of modernity. And yet here was another drift, going against the uprooted grain. For all his urbanity, 'who once strode / head-high in the forum', Mahon's Ovid is grounded in the weather and wildlife of the Danube delta. A shift of translation takes us from the rainy abandonment of the northern Irish coast to the Danube delta and its Scythian wind where Ovid has to button his sheepskin. I still delight in the speaker's credentials as a naturalist, writing a study of fish of the Black Sea (the *Halieutica*) and celebrating the birdlife of the area. When I read the moment on the dunes, with the poet 'listening hard / to the uninhibited // virtuosity of a lark', I am fully invested.

Reaching even further, in a deft display of concision and connection, the metamorphic reeds of the delta move from the tale of Syrinx's transformation and get enlisted into a story for our time of environmental plunder; then, as raw material for paper, they are raised even beyond this to a Zen-inspired lament for the desecration of the page by upstart art: 'it speaks volumes / no one will ever write.'

When I return to it now, given the scope and virtuosity of all the later work, 'Ovid in Tomis' seems exemplary, with its masterful focus of a sensibility that would sustain Derek Mahon as a poet for almost the next forty years.

Kinsale

The kind of rain we knew is a thing of the past —
deep-delving, dark, deliberate you would say,
browsing on spire and bogland; but today
our sky-blue slates are steaming in the sun,
our yachts tinkling and dancing in the bay
like racehorses. We contemplate at last
shining windows, a future forbidden to no one.

Eamon Grennan
Kinsale

Short as it is, 'Kinsale' is a revealingly rich compendium of some of Derek Mahon's characteristic habits as a poet. In what follows I'll take a rapid line by line read through it.

Kinsale: a harbour, a space of settlement between land and sea, a place of arrival or departure. In a wandering life (the North, Dublin, England, London, Paris, New York), Kinsale (where he lived for a while in the 1980s) represented a 'safe harbour' where he made his chosen home for the last twenty years of his life.

> *The kind of rain we knew is a thing of the past . . .*

Rain, presumably Irish rain. I'm caught by that 'we'. We're in the speaking mind of an observer with a generalizing, mildly philosophic bent. As often, Mahon is at ease, speaking for a community, for a shared point of view.

> *. . . deep-delving, dark, deliberate you would say . . .*

The *you* here could be particular or general. What strikes me most, however, is the layering levels of diction and their various implications: 'dark' can be practical, metaphorical, emotional all at once, while 'deep-delving' shifts from common into old-fashioned, more 'literary' language, and the following phrase is all colloquial ease. All three language units make this a very animated rain indeed, showing the kind of 'thickening' I love in Mahon's work, rhythmically moving between relaxed and regular iambic — roughly pentameter — lines, with some striking enjambments.

> *. . . browsing on spire and bogland; but today . . .*

Again the surprise of diction, the sense of so much going on. 'Browsing' is a lovely surprise, with gentler implications than the rain has in the preceding alliterative line. Then 'spire and bogland' carry on the sense of the variously divided island of Ireland with their different shorthand cultural and geographical resonances. There's a turn, then, moving us from past to present, pivoting on that 'but':

> *. . . our sky-blue slates are steaming in the sun . . .*

Suddenly we're in a fresh new world where dark has given way to light, to sunshine on wet slates and the lively sky-blue energies of air: the dark rain rising as luminous steam. In addition, that rather forbidding spire and bogland have through those roof-slates become an image of domestic security, of peace, the rain itself maybe even transformed to the 'gentle rain from heaven' that reveals 'the quality of mercy'.

> *. . . our yachts tinkling and dancing in the bay . . .*

This line brings us into a zone of purely lyrical description: of the buoyantly, physically alive yachts in Kinsale bay, from which the poem advances into its highest gear with another startling turn:

> *. . . like racehorses. We contemplate at last . . .*

As readers we're drawn from the lively harbour yachts to the excitement of a racetrack, whence we're transported, surprisingly, into the realm of *contemplation*. It is a word, a state, towards which all these lines have been driving (as very often happens in a Mahon poem): a movement towards lightly handled philosophic contemplation. For me, indeed, his work so often speaks and sings in the key of contemplation — a word that not only contains in its etymology the notion of deep *attention*, but also the notion of a *place* from which to practise such attention, that enables it. A place, in other words, such as Kinsale was for this most contemplative of poets.

And so we can move to the final line, to what contemplation in this case finally reveals:

> *. . . shining windows, a future forbidden to no one.*

As readers we may recognize at last how the whole poem is a journey of private contemplation, begun in the shadows of a dark, rain-drenched divided landscape, but travelling on to an optimistic act of hope, bright and visionary in scope. As an ending it seems to summarize so much in Mahon's whole way of taking on the world with total honesty: always admitting to its mingled nature but so often reaching, too, through his muscularly capacious imagination, to a state that may be summarized in one simple, emblematic idea: despite the worst, everything is going to be all right. This, of course, is the title of an earlier, by now iconic Mahon poem, the first line of which also contains (in the context of the ordinary world) the word contemplate: 'How should I not be glad to contemplate / the clouds clearing beyond the dormer window . . . '

In 'Kinsale', then, those dark divisions at the start give way at last to a contemplated, visionary, hopeful, unified *future forbidden to no one*. And the poet, and his poem, can rest there. For the moment.

Dawn at St Patrick's

for Terence Brown

There is an old
statue in the courtyard
that weeps, like Niobe, its sorrow in stone.
The griefs of the ages she has made her own.
Her eyes are rain-washed but not hard,
her body is covered in mould,
the garden overgrown.

One by one
the first lights come on,
those that haven't been on all night.
Christmas, the harshly festive, has come and gone.
No snow, but the rain pours down
in the first hour before dawn,
before daylight.

Swift's home
for 'fools and mad' has become
the administrative block. Much there
has remained unchanged for many a long year —
stairs, chairs, Georgian windows shafting light and dust,
radiantly white the marble bust
of the satirist;

but the real
hospital is a cheerful
modern extension at the back
hung with restful reproductions of Klee, Dufy and Braque.
Television, Russian fiction, snooker with the staff,
a snifter of Lucozade, a paragraph
of *Newsweek* or the *Daily Mail*

are my daily routine
during the festive season.
They don't lock the razors here
as in Bowditch Hall. We have remained upright —
though, to be frank, the Christmas dinner scene,
with grown men in their festive gear,
was a sobering sight.

I watch the last
planes of the year go past,
silently climbing a cloud-lit sky.
Earthbound, soon I'll be taking a train to Cork
and trying to get back to work
at my sea-lit, fort-view desk
in the turfsmoky dusk.

Meanwhile,
next door, a visiting priest
intones to a faithful dormitory.
I sit on my Protestant bed, a make-believe existentialist,
and stare at the clouds of unknowing. We style,
as best we may, our private destiny;
or so it seems to me

as I chew my thumb
and try to figure out
what brought me to my present state —
an 'educated man', a man of consequence, no bum
but one who has hardly grasped what life is about,
if anything. My children, far away,
don't know where I am today,

in a Dublin asylum
with a paper whistle and a mince pie,
my bits and pieces making a home from home.

I pray to the rain clouds that they never come
where their lost father lies, that their mother thrives
    and that I
may measure up to them
before I die.

Soon a new year
will be here demanding, as before,
modest proposals, resolute resolutions, a new leaf,
new leaves. This is the story of my life,
the story of all lives everywhere,
mad fools wherever we are,
in here or out there.

Light and sane
I shall walk down to the train,
into that world whose sanity we know,
like Swift, to be a fiction and a show.
The clouds part, the rain ceases, the sun
casts now upon everyone
its ancient shadow.

Medbh McGuckian
Dawn at St Patrick's

I will never forget the Queen's conference in the Elmwood Hall at which all guest poets were ensconced on stage preparing their wares when Derek Mahon, hitherto looking as if butter wouldn't melt in his mouth, announced in his dulcet baritones that he was only going to read six poems, each of them referring to a county in Northern Ireland, beginning with County Antrim, which was of course what the conference was all about. There was none of us could upstage that cleverest of chess moves.

Nearly all of Mahon's poems are set at a specific time of day or year, in a designated exhaustively described place, often dedicated in conversation to a fellow poet or friend. Often they are inspired by European paintings which define a moment closer to home, or they are free translations 'after' a French or Russian source. Of all his contemporary rhymsters he is the strictest: metre, stanza and line flowing effortlessly, while the subject matter is anything but effortless.

As classical a scholar as Seamus Heaney departing this world with 'Noli timere' on the lips of his phone, no matter how many times I come across Derek Mahon's abstract/concrete yokings I still have to look up, for example, 'esurient sea', its playfulness. It was not nonsense but rather all great fun to him. I recall him in Greenwich Village, in drooping overcoat and what Ciaran used to call rather disparagingly 'mutton dummies', pointing out Latin or Greek mottoes around the necks of buildings to Paul and me. It was both erudite and entertaining.

The word 'dark' recurs constantly, though we are never left in it. A cliché embalmed in each poem is made to spin like a kaleidoscope. For strictly speaking I am already dead, your ashes will not stir. Light is refracted in a glass of beer, as if through a church window. Give or take a day or two my days are numbered. The lives we might have led. He has changed into the shade that pleased him best. There will be dying, there will be dying, but there is no need to go into that . . .

He finds himself unnerved, his talents on the shelf, slumped in a deckchair, full of pills. All the time I have my doubts about this verse-making. I who know nothing go to teach, a strange child with a taste for verse. My consolation will be the unspoilt paper when you have gone. The new thing that must come out of the scrunched Budweiser can. Perhaps I am already dead and dreaming my vigilance, tranced in a prescience of the life to come. An only child launches a toy canoe.

Tolstoy says in 'What is Art?' that true art is modest, a display of virtuosity is a sign of bad art. 'Dawn at St Patrick's' I single out for its modesty compared with 'A Disused Shed in Co. Wexford' or 'A Garage in Co. Cork' although it is composed to the same formula. We come closer to his actual experience here as he nears the end of a drying-out period where a 'snifter of Lucozade' is a Christmas luxury. He is essentially low rather than high here, and while it is a Song before Sunrise or Aubade, for muse he has only the depressed famine figure in the yard, the old woman of Beare, the Shan Van Bhoct. It may be he has not slept, is afflicted with insomnia.

He creates his environment with his usual Dereksterity, placing himself stoically in Swift's home for those dying at the top. Whose bust by contrast is clinically pure. Mahon loads the words 'cheerful' and 'restful' with heavy irony, being a satirist himself. He sums up his reading matter and entertainment as conventionally undisturbing. But the mention of 'razors' understates the actual mental danger he might not have survived. The season he describes has been not festive, but *harshly* festive and unavoidably sobering. His departure is imminent, his desk beckons with freedom, while Mass murmurs for the Catholic inmates highlighting his solitude.

He is at a loss to understand his predicament, which he understands only too well, caricaturing it as comic, a paper whistle and a mince pie. Another frequent word is 'measure', meaning here to recover status. This is the story of my life. Elsewhere he is one of the few Irish or Northern Irish voices to refer to the political prisoners in any way positively:

> *I stared each night*
> *at a glow of yellow light*
> *over the water where the interned sat tight . . .*
> — 'Craigvara House'

A map of Ireland or indeed America and further could be plotted with the sites he lends his aura to. Loneliness is courted, sanity an illusion, he is the lost master of the tongue-in-cheek refrain:

> *I am just going outside and may be some time.*

> *Everything is going to be all right.*

Global Village

This morning, from beyond abandoned piers
where the great liners docked in former years,
a foghorn echoes in deserted sheds
known to Hart Crane, and in our vigilant beds.
No liners now, nothing but ice and grime,
a late flame flickering on Brodsky St. News time
in the global village — Ethiopian drought,
famine, whole nations, races, evicted even yet,
rape victim and blind beggar at the gate —
the real-time images which will be screened tonight
on CNN and *The McNeil-Lehrer News Hour*,
the sense of being right there on the spot —
a sense I get right here that Gansevoort
has 'no existence, natural or real, apart
from its being perceived by the understanding'. Not
that I seriously doubt the reality of the Hudson Bar
and Diner; but the skills of Venturi, Thompson, Rowse
that can make post-modern a 19th-century warehouse
and those of Hollywood *film noir* have combined
to create virtual realities in the mind
so the real thing tells us what we already know
behind the signs. Obviously I don't mean
to pen yet one more craven European
paean to the States, nor would you expect me to,
not being a yuppie in a pinstripe suit
but an Irish bohemian even as you are too
though far from the original 'Ballroom of Romance',
far too from your posh convent school in France.
Out here in the clear existential light
I miss the half-tones we're accustomed to:
an amateur immigrant, sure I like the corny
humanism and car-stickers — 'I♥NY' —
and yet remain sardonic and un-*chic*,
an undesirable resident alien on this shore,
a face in the crowd in this offshore boutique

inscribed with the ubiquitous comic-strip blob-speak —
LOVE ONE ANOTHER, RESIST INSIPID RHYME —
exposed in thunderstorms, as once before,
and hoping to draw some voltage one more time.

Ailbhe Ní Ghearbhuigh
Global Village

The city demands our attention. The foghorn that sounds at the opening of 'Global Village' announces the immediacy of 'this morning' in New York. Sure, the same foghorn has echoed throughout history too, it evokes arrivals and tired, poor, huddled masses. But here the sound blasts us into the present: 'the sense of being right there on the spot'. It is difficult to escape that feeling in New York, better to embrace it.

The bedlam of living is documented throughout *The Hudson Letter* (now 'New York Time'). In this section the tumult is both local and international. Even events at a geographic remove acquire the illusion of proximity here, in their compilation for the *McNeil-Lehrer News Hour*. If there is unrest in the world beyond the apartment it seems to augment the sense of introspection in the poet.

There is an intimacy in the letter form, as we eavesdrop on Mahon's unguarded musings, the gentle teasing of the lover to whom he writes, and his sardonic assessment of himself. The poem is, to some extent, a portrait of the artist in the city, an impression of the poet in reflective mode amidst the din of Lower Manhattan.

The familiarity of New York — a cityscape known to us forever, seemingly, from screens small and large — results in a kind of sensory overload, a hyperrealism, creating 'virtual realities in the mind'. Does anything exist in the absence of its being perceived? The poet considers Bishop Berkeley's assertion that 'no existence, natural or real, apart / from its being perceived by the understanding'. Máirtín Ó Direáin wrote about Berkeley's ideas, too, but in relation to his home place of Aran, the very rocks of which may fade from existence without anyone to behold them. Unlike Inis Mór, nothing is in such jeopardy in New York: everything exists because it is observed and grasped, haggled over and consumed.

Like many others I was 'an amateur immigrant' over there for a while. And, like Mahon, I lived just a couple of blocks from the Hudson, though I was there twenty years later and lived much further north, in West Harlem. The closest I used to get to the Hudson was taking the 1 train as it slowly rose from subterranean grot to daylight, apartment blocks and glimpses of river around 125th Street.

I could tell you a hundred insipid anecdotes that would hardly distil the essence of the place, nor capture its 'clear existential light'. And although I wouldn't want 'to pen yet one more craven European / paean to the States', that is not to say I haven't. I'll join the chorus of those who proclaim New York a place like no other. Reading 'Global Village' I recall my own sense of serene aloneness — and occasional self-consciousness — as I sat with a notebook and pen in Bryant Park, in downtown cafés or in my own studio uptown trying to generate a poem, 'to draw some voltage one more time'.

Alien Nation

These chronic homeless are mostly single adults who have given
up seeking help because they feel the 'system' has given up on
them and is largely unresponsive to their needs. Many are sub-
stance abusers . . . Getting high or drunk may be the only way
they know of alleviating their pain and disappointment.
       — *What You Can Do to Help the Homeless*

RX GOTHAM DRUG GAY CRUISES SONY LIQUORS MARLBORO
ADULT VIDEO XXX BELSHAZZAR DEATH IS BACK
IGLESIA ADVENTISTA DEL 7MO. DIA . . .
We come upon them in the restless dark
in the moon-shadow of the World Trade Centre
with Liberty's torch glimmering over the water,
glued to a re-run of *The Exterminator*
on a portable TV in a corner of Battery Park
(some have park views, others sleep in the park),
and think how sensible the alternative polity
beneath the ostensible, pharaonic city
glimpsed through rain or dust from an expressway —
the old clothes, packing cases and auto trunks
seen everywhere from here to the South Bronx,
its population growing by the week, by the day,
oblivious to our chaos theories and data banks,
from the Port Authority Bus Terminal to JFK
and farther afield, in freight-yard and loading bay,
gull-screaming landfill, stripped trailer and boxcar,
the gap increasing between the penthouse tower
and the desert of cinderblock and razor wire
behind the Ritz-Carlton or Holiday Inn.
We are all survivors in this rough terrain;
I know you and you me, you wretched buggers,
and I've no problem calling you my brothers
for I too have been homeless and in detox
with BAAAD niggaz 'n' crack hoes on the rocks.
Blown here like particles from an exploding sun,

we are all far from home, be our home still
a Chicago slum, a house under the Cave Hill
or a trailer parked in a field above Cushendun.
Clutching our bits and pieces, arrogant in dereliction,
we are all out there, filling the parks and streets
with our harsh demand: 'Sleep faster, we need the sheets!'
Now off to your high loft in the disco night,
young faces glittering under trippy light,
smoke red and yellow where the doctor spins
high-octane decks among the boogie bins.
An ocean breeze, flower-scented, soft and warm,
blows downtown where we part in the night air;
a Haitian driver, mordant as Baudelaire,
whisks me up Hudson St. in a thunderstorm.

Ciaran Berry
Alien Nation

I like to imagine Derek Mahon 'bopping up Bleecker', as he puts it in 'Beauty and the Beast', another poem from *The Hudson Letter* (or 'New York Time' as it appears in *New Collected Poems*). An amateur immigrant, an undesirable 'resident alien', an Irish Bohemian in Greenwich Village, where the Bohemians are long gone. Mahon's New York is one of graffiti, billboards, and dive bars. It's a 24-hr film set, what he calls elsewhere 'this autistic slammer'. He moves through it in a perpetual state of sensory overload. A poet who never sleeps in a city that never sleeps.

Like Lorca, whose *Poet in New York* grew from his time at Columbia University, Mahon is often appalled by what he sees — extreme wealth and extreme poverty, waste and indifference. Unlike Lorca he manages to register these phenomena with levity as well as gravity, a kind of bemused amusement that runs parallel to the horror.

'Alien Nation' begins with an epigraph as do so many of the poems in the sequence, the poet drawing on a list of co-conspirators that includes everyone from John Keats to Eartha Kitt. Then it's advertisements and snippets of graffiti, another source of material that crops up frequently, before we're into the poem proper. It's like he's playing with a transistor radio. Mahon fiddles the dial and brings us a quote from here, a commercial from there, before he finally settles on a station.

He takes us to the World Trade Centre and the Statue of Liberty, pointing to the contrast between the fantasies these symbols foster and the realities that undercut such fantasies. He wants us to read his image of those homeless 'glued to a re-run of *The Exterminator* / on a portable TV in a corner of Battery Park' in the shadow of that hub of commerce and that statue inscribed with the words 'give me your tired, your poor'. The choice of film is deliberate, and even the name of the park becomes part of Mahon's scheme. His New York is a place where 'some have park views' while 'others sleep in the park', with 'the gap increasing between the penthouse tower / and the desert of cinderblock and razor wire'.

Addiction, too, is never far away, and the speaker's own experience gives him a deep sense of empathy for those 'wretched buggers' he has no problem calling 'my brothers', having himself been, he tells us, if hyperbolically, 'homeless and in detox'. He displays a keen eye for the predicament of the destitute, seeing their displacement as kin to his own in this city, where so many are 'far from home', whether home is 'a Chicago slum, a house under the Cave Hill / or a trailer parked in a field above Cushendun'.

It's around this point, too, that Mahon's revisions of the poem as it originally appeared in *The Hudson Letter* become more pointed. Gone in the 'New York Time' version is that reworking of perhaps his most famous line, 'a strange child with a taste for verse' from 'Courtyards in Delft', to 'a strange child with a taste for vorse'. Gone, too, the trudging through the snow at 3 a.m. The punning patter of a panhandler who pleads, 'Spare a thought, friend; spare a dime, bud; spare the price of a Bud' is also omitted.

Instead of these moments we get a more up-to-date sketch of the New York nightlife. The city's denizens are off to a 'high loft in the disco night' rather than the quiet corner of some watering hole. Instead of that lone figure traipsing to the Lion's Head, McKenna's or the White Horse, we get 'young faces glittering under trippy light' as a DJ spins dance music 'among the boogie bins'.

In the later version, Mahon is less in the picture. He stands outside this party life as he stands outside the 'heavy metal' rocking 'the discothèques' in his earlier poem 'Rock Music'. And what comes across more powerfully as a result is our sense of the poet as alien, and of this alien nation as no country for old or even middle-aged men.

A Bangor Requiem

We stand — not many of us — in a new cemetery
on a cold hillside in Co. Down, your few
last friends and relatives, declining too,
and stare at an open grave or out to sea,
the lough half-hidden by great drifts of rain.
Only a few months since you were snug at home
in a bungalow glow, keeping provincial time
in the chimney corner, *News Letter* and *Woman's Own*
on your knee, wool-gathering by Plato's firelight,
a grudging flicker of flame on anthracite.
Inactive since your husband died, your chief
concern the 'appearances' that ruled your life
in a neighbourhood of bay windows and stiff
gardens shivering in the salt sea air,
the sunburst ideogram on door and gate,
you knew the secret history of needlework,
bread bin and laundry basket awash with light.
The figure in the *Republic* returns to the cave,
a Dutch interior where cloud shadows move,
to examine the intimate spaces, chest and drawer,
the lavender in the linen, the savings book,
the kitchen table silent with nobody there.
Shall we say the patience of an angel? No,
not unless angels be thought anxious too.
God knows you had reason to be; and yet
with your wise monkeys and 'Dresden' figurines,
your junk chinoiserie and coy pastoral scenes,
you too were an artist, a rage-for-order freak
setting against a man's aesthetic of cars and golf
your ornaments and other breakable stuff.
Just visible from your window the 6th-century
abbey church of Columbanus and Malachi,
'light of the world' once in the monastic ages,
home of antiphonary and the golden pages
of radiant scripture; though you had your own

idea of the beautiful, not unrelated to Tolstoy
but formed in a tough city of ships and linen,
Harland & Wolff, Mackie's, Gallaher's, Lyle & Kinahan
and your own York St. Flax Spinning Co. Ltd.;
daft musicals at the Curzon and the Savoy.

   Beneath a Castilian sky, at a great mystic's rococo tomb,
I thought of the plain Protestant fatalism of home.
Remember 1690; prepare to meet thy God —
I grew up among washing lines and grey skies,
pictures of Brookeborough on the gable ends,
revolvers, RUC, 'B' Specials, law-'n'-order,
a hum of drums above the summer glens
shattering the twilight over lough water
in a violent post-industrial sunset blaze
while you innocently hummed 'South of the Border',
'On a Slow Boat to China', 'Beyond the Blue Horizon'.
Little soul, the body's guest and companion,
this is a cold epitaph from your only son,
the wish genuine if the tone ambiguous.
Oh, I can love you now that you're dead and gone
to the many mansions in your mother's house;
all artifice stripped away, we give you back to nature
but something of you, perhaps the incurable ache
of art, goes with me as I travel south
past misty drumlins, shining lanes to the shore,
above the Mournes a final helicopter,
sun-showers and rainbows all the way through Louth,
cottages buried deep in ivy and rhododendron,
ranch houses, dusty palms, blue skies of the republic . . .

Colm Tóibín
A Bangor Requiem

While an elegy, a lament, a poem to mark a death, usually begins with a hushed tone, Derek Mahon's 'A Bangor Requiem' starts with a spondee, the two sounds — 'We stand' — firm, solid, assertive, which the next phrase, an aside, sets out to wrongfoot. 'We stand' is made almost ironic by 'not many of us'; it is no longer a position of strength.

The cemetery is 'new'; the hillside is 'cold'. The friends are 'few'. There is no buried rhythm in these opening lines to suggest sorrow or grief or regret. The dead woman is not addressed as Patrick Kavanagh addresses his mother at the opening of 'In Memory of My Mother': 'I do not think of you lying in the wet clay / Of a Monaghan graveyard.' The opening line is not in soft-sounding iambic pentameter, as in Seamus Heaney's 'When all the others were away at Mass'. The fourth line 'the lough half-hidden by great drifts of rain' does not have the sense of disruption we get in the opening of Seán Ó Ríordáin's 'Adhlacadh mo Mháthar': 'Grian an Mheithimh in úllghort, / Is siosarnach i síoda an tráthnóna.'

The rhymes are mostly off-rhymes or side-rhymes. They mark line endings, but they don't create any easy rhythm or pattern. The tone is a voice in conversation, someone stating some facts. It is not as though emotion is being held back, or implied in the poem's diction or in the figures it invokes. The 'stiff / gardens shivering in the salt sea air' are not metaphors; they are gardens. The 'sunburst ideogram' is also itself. But these figures accumulate to create a sense that sunlight and shivering cold are involved in a mild battle, but nothing grand, nothing dramatic.

The poem does not move out of ordinary domestic space, the space inhabited by the dead woman. Instead, ordinary domestic space takes on the subdued glow of intimacy, as a Dutch interior might in a painting. If the 'bread bin' and 'laundry basket' are 'awash with light', it is restrained light. The mute phenomena are to be listed, not celebrated or asked to hold more tension than they might. Angels are invoked, but at first they belong in the cliché 'the patience of an angel'. Plato's cave becomes a domestic space.

Instead of angst here, there is anxiety. Instead of art, there are 'figurines'. It is as if Derek Mahon had found a style that was almost prose, and grafted it onto an attitude towards material where strong emotion is tempered by domestic ordinariness, where nothing is allowed to shine too brightly, where feeling is kept in check or bathed in irony; where pathos is kept to a minimum.

The poem sees the mother with clarity and sympathy; it is gently trying to bring her into the poet's orbit, or allow the writer, the son, as an artist too, to move into hers.

In the section of the poem when he writes 'you too were an artist' Derek Mahon does something strange, he invites his mother to inhabit the aura of certain of his own poems from the past, as if she and they might once have been acquainted, or she might have been an aspect of their source. She is a 'rage-for-order freak', just as Mahon, in an earlier poem, creates a version of himself as 'a poet indulging / his wretched rage for order'. Also, he can visualize his mother among ornaments and ordinary things, just as he in his poem 'The Mute Phenomena' will declare: 'God is alive and lives under a stone' and exalt the turnip, cutlery, the brick wall, the lost hubcap.

Mahon allows images of light into the poem. The abbey, just visible from his mother's window, can be connected to 'light of the world' in the monastic ages, and it is home to 'the golden pages / of radiant scripture'. But the poem resists making too much of this. It wants to return to the actual life the dead woman has lived and what she has enjoyed ('daft musicals at the Curzon and the Savoy') rather than bathe in light that a poem has made for her.

And then the poem breaks. Mahon imagines the home

scene from abroad, contemplating the 'washing lines and grey skies' and moving then into matters that have caused misery in Northern Ireland ('revolvers, RUC, 'B' Specials') and setting them against the tunes his mother 'innocently hummed': 'South of the Border', 'On a Slow Boat to China', 'Beyond the Blue Horizon'.

Up to now the poem wallows in the ordinary. Even when it includes the lines about the 'hum of drums . . . shattering the twilight over lough water / in a violent post-industrial sunset blaze', the world invoked is visible. Twelve lines into this second part of the poem, however, having listed the songs his mother hummed, ordinary tunes of the times, Mahon seeks pay-off for the minor key in which he has been writing. His insistence on keeping things down to earth now earns him the right to see what might happen if he lifted his gaze.

He moves carefully from the physical into the spiritual, calling the dead woman 'Little soul', and addressing her directly, plainly: 'this is a cold epitaph from your only son, / the wish genuine if the tone ambiguous'.

The poem regularly returns to speaking plainly, replacing the sonorous, comforting language of lament with clear-eyed fact, however hard to register, including the line: 'Oh, I can love you now that you're dead and gone.'

While the coldness of the tone can be noted and felt there is an overtone that is not only modest but also true, or desperate not to say anything that is untrue. The poem is a tribute to clear statement, emotional precision, tonal guardedness.

While Mahon has been careful to indulge no soft-eyed hyperbole in this elegy he has moved his mother from being 'snug' in 'bungalow glow, keeping provincial time' to being 'Little soul, the body's guest and companion'. Her ornaments, her musicals, her songs have taken on 'perhaps the incurable ache / of art'. And that is what travels with him as he moves south, as he notes 'a final helicopter' over the Mournes, and then into Louth, under 'blue skies of the republic'.

Just as in the poem 'Afterlives' in which Derek Mahon ponders 'what is meant by home', 'A Bangor Requiem' faces the question of what is meant by elegy, what a requiem should sound like. In his poem 'all artifice [is] stripped away'. The battle is between plain speech and some hints at transcendence. No matter which side wins, 'the tone [is] ambiguous'. The power of the poem comes from the hesitancy that breaks through the sureness, from allowing the glow to move from the domestic, the contained, into some more numinous space, but all the time eschewing easy emotion or an easy metrical system, trying to pay homage not only to what has been clearly seen, but also to what is 'just visible' or, now, after her death, scrupulously imagined.

Shapes and Shadows

— William Scott, oil on canvas,
Ulster Museum

The kitchens would grow bright
in blue frames; outside, still
harbour and silent cottages
from a time of shortages,
shapes deft and tranquil,
black kettle and black pot.

Too much the known structures
those simple manufactures,
communion of frying pans,
skinny beans and spoons,
colander and fish slice
in a polished interior space.

But tension of hand and heart
abstracted the growing art
to a dissonant design
and a rich dream of paint,
on the grim basic plan
a varied white pigment

knifed and scrubbed, in one
corner an enigmatic
study in mahogany;
beige-biscuit left; right
a fat patch of white,
bread and milk in agony.

Rough brushwork here, thick
but vague; for already
behind these there loom
shades of the prehistoric,

ghosts of colour and form,
furniture, function, body —

as if to announce the death
of preconception and myth
and start again on the fresh
first morning of the world
with snow, ash, whitewash,
limestone, mother-of-pearl,

bleach, paper, soap, foam
and cold kitchen cream,
to find in the nitty-gritty
of surfaces and utensils
the shadow of a presence,
a long-sought community.

Sara Berkeley
Shapes and Shadows

In the summer of 1988, when I was a J-1 student in California, Derek Mahon sent me a postcard of Francis Bacon's *Dog*. On the back he wrote 'Artist's impression of ould dog overcome by an excess of Modern Art'. Also in the envelope were a few American quarters which he mentioned I could use to call my friends when I got to San Francisco.

Mahon's deprecation of modern art was typical of his habit of maligning things and then writing exquisite poems about them. This would be true of 'Shapes and Shadows', a poem he wrote around 1990 about William Scott's abstract painting on show in the Ulster Museum. For someone who made fun of modern painting, the delicacy and care with which he wrote about it give a glimpse into his complexity, his wicked sense of humour and his consummate art.

Giorgio Morandi said, 'Nothing is more abstract than reality.' Mahon is a poet who largely wrote very plainly about life. 'The lines flow from the hand unbidden,' he wrote in 'Everything Is Going to Be All Right', 'and the hidden source is the watchful heart'. 'Shapes and Shadows' takes a leap from his usual style. It is a flight, unexpected and glorious, into the painting, the paint, and ultimately something that humans seem to yearn for with their art in all its forms: 'a long-sought community'.

Having appraised Scott's painting he describes in luscious detail what he sees there. Faced with what a bystander might call a collection of shapes, Mahon finds a 'rich dream of paint'. Against the 'grim basic plan', he describes 'a fat patch of white, / bread and milk in agony'.

This is not just the poet extrapolating wildly. Mahon's vision is much deeper. In the 'rough brushwork . . . thick / but vague,' he reaches back in time: 'behind these there loom / shades of the prehistoric', and then he reaches forward again, and then he settles in the present moment with his fierce and fearless clarity:

as if to announce the death
of preconception and myth
and start again on the fresh
first morning of the world
with snow, ash, whitewash,
limestone, mother-of-pearl,

bleach, paper, soap, foam
and cold kitchen cream . . .

I was lucky enough to be Derek's poetry student during his 1986 tenure as Writer Fellow at Trinity College. You might think I memorized plentiful nuggets of writing wisdom, but you would be wrong. I remember his tenacious attention to form and discipline: he made me write my first villanelle and I grumbled the whole way through. I remember how he relentlessly instructed me to immerse myself in other poets. 'Read Elizabeth Bishop and keep in touch,' he wrote on another postcard. But what I remember most about the man was his kindness. 'Mind now,' he would end his letters with. A curiously gentle farewell from a man so reserved.

My summer in California must have had its unhappy moments that I wrote to him about, because he replied to me on August 3rd: 'You have nothing to fear and everything to look forward to; life will be kind to you because you are kind to life . . . You have not a damn thing to worry about, so long as you read Bishop. Never mind Williams, except 'El Hombre'; and don't be intimidated by American cultural imperialism. A lot of nonsense really; we are the ones who know, so come back soon and give me a shout, *gnädige Fräulein*. Enjoy Disneyland meanwhile: it's only a joke, after all.'

Harbour Lights

*And I ... a mere newcomer whose ancestors had inhabited
the earth so briefly that my presence was almost anachronistic.*
— Rachel Carson, *The Edge of the Sea*

It's one more sedative evening in Co. Cork.
The house is quiet and the world is dark
while the Bush gang are doing it to Iraq.
The flesh is weary and I've read the books;
nothing but lies and nonsense on the box
whose light-dot vanishes with a short whine
leaving only a grey ghost in the machine.
Slick boats click at the quayside down below
the drowsy bungalows of the well-to-do;
late light illuminates the closing pub,
shop window, leisure centre and sailing club,
exhausted cars tucked up in their garages,
rabbits and foxes, birds dumb in the hedges;
midsummer light shifting its general blaze
sets in a secret thicket of hazel trees,
on garden sheds and lined pre-Cambrian rock
red as the wavy roof tiles of Languedoc.
Re-reading history page by lamplit page,
imagining the lost poems of Iníon Dubh,
I could be living here in another age
except at weekends when the bikes converge.
Blow-in asylum and dormitory of privilege,
its dreamy woods are straight out of Chekhov,
quaint gardens made for 19th-century love;
transnational, the skies are Indian skies,
the harbour lights Chinese or Japanese;
and certain thatchy corners the gull sees
keep the last traces of the bardic phase,
straw spaces echoing to disconsolate cries.

Get out more? I prefer to watch by starlight
the London plane, a galaxy in flight,
night-shining cloud, a ghost ship among stars,
and the light fading from our western shores.
It's now that the high spirits begin to drop,
remembering buried errors and wasted time;
but in the morning when the sun comes up
there will be snail mail with its pearly gleam
and a gruff husky scratching on the gravel,
young people chattering as in a Russian novel,
sky-shining roofs where smoky notions rise,
back yards where the drainpipes soliloquize,
a wood-shriek as a whining saw spins free
and the wild soul flies from a stricken tree.
Alive to voices and, to my own surprise,
up with the lark, up with the June sunrise,
I study the visible lines of tidal flow,
the spidery leaves alight with sweat and dew,
doors blazing primary colours, blue and red,
phone-lines at angles against piling cloud.

Go wandering with your stick on the back road,
you start with a ruined convent school, a tough
chough cursing you from a lichen-speckled roof;
organic fields to the left; and, to the right,
the mud basin of one more building site.
Startling how fast a thing can integrate:
beneath those tiles some immigrant teenager
will write the secret poetry of the future.
Sun-ripples on the trout-shimmering Bandon River
where on a clear day you can see for ever;
a flash of foam like Gray's *Great Wave at Sète*,
alternate light and shade on the shut eyes,
the untaken photograph and the unwritten phrase;

woof of a terrier, crash of a fluttering wing,
the bird-voiced tinkle of a hidden spring.
Now, note that white sail where a dinghy moves,
a raw strand where Cúchulainn fought the waves,
a writhing Daphne hawthorn, hands and hair
mute but articulate in the Atlantic air,
chained in the ivy strings that bind her there
while somebody takes shape in the heat haze:
a young woman in tracksuit and running shoes.
A cloud covers the sun and a quick shower
scribbles with many pencils on the estuary,
the coves, the beaches and the open sea,
sub-tropical wave-light where it calmly roars
at dark soul cottages with their shining doors,
the docks in fierce, eye-straining definition,
each thing distinct but in oblique relation;
the *faux* schooner bearing a famous name,
a pocket cruise ship like a video game.

    Back at the house revisit the dark grove
of baths, old cars and fridges, while above
a withered orchard the slow cloud-cranes move
in the empty silence where a myth might start —
flute-note, god-word — the first whisper of art
withdrawn in its integrity, in its own
obscurity, for not everything need be known.
Magic survives only where blind profit,
so quick on the uptake, takes no notice of it
for ours is a crude culture dazed with money,
a flighty future that would ditch its granny.
The orchard withers but the birds sing on
through the long morning, and in the afternoon
you watch clouds gather and disperse, paint dry,
and listen patiently to the wasp and fly.

But everything is noticed, everything known
in the 'knowledge era', advertised as the one
without precedent; though in late middle age,
striving to tame the Yeatsian lust and rage,
claim the now disgraceful privilege
of living part-time in a subversive past:
'... fall and are built again'; nor is this the last,
for the tough nuts, imagining you fortunate,
will aim to get you with their curious hate.
Try the Blue Haven, its interior bright
with port-holes and chronometers, spare parts;
winking in turn, a frieze of lighthouse charts.

Lady, whose shrine stands on the promontory
above the fancy golf course, taking inventory
of vapour trails and nuclear submarines,
keep close watch on our flight paths and sea lanes,
our tourist coaches and our slot machines,
the cash dynamic and the natural gas.
Your arbour stands there as it always has,
secret and shy above these baffling shores
and the white-winged oceanic water table.
A short path and a tumbler of fresh flowers,
a cup of dusty water, bead and pebble,
the salt-whipped plaster of your serious head,
an azure radiance in your tiny shed
gazing out over the transatlantic cable
with a chipped eye towards Galicia and the Azores.

I toy with cloud thoughts as an alternative
to the global shit storm that we know and love,
but unsustainable levels of aviation
have complicated this vague resolution;
for even clouds are gobbled up by the sun,
not even the ethereal clouds are quite immune:

these too will be marketed if it can be done.
I was here once before, though, at Kinsale
with the mad chiefs, and lived to tell the tale;
I too froze in the hills, first of the name
in Monaghan, great my pride and great my shame —
or was it a slander that we tipped them off,
old Hugh asking a quart of Powers from Taaffe?
Does it matter now? Oh yes, it still matters;
strange currents circulate in these calm waters
though we don't mention them, we talk instead
of the new golf course out at the Old Head.
What have I achieved? Oh, little enough, God knows:
some dubious verse and some ephemeral prose;
as for the re-enchantment of the sky,
that option was never really going to fly
but it's too late to do much about it now
except to trust in the contumacious few
who aren't afraid to point to an obvious truth,
and the frank stare of unpredictable youth.

A buoy nods faintly in the harbour mouth
as I slope down to the front for a last walk
and watch trawlers disgorging at the dock
in the loud work-glow of a Polish freighter,
dark oil drums and fish boxes on the quay,
winches and ropes, intestines of the sea
alive with the stench of pre-historic water.
I've noted codgers, when the day is done,
sitting in easy rows in the evening sun
before the plate-faced rising moon creates
a sphere of influence where thought incubates
with midnight oil and those old harbour lights,
'the harbour lights that once brought you to me'.
White page, dark world; wave theory; moon and pines:
thin as an aspirin that vast surface shines,

the pits and heights in intimate close-up,
her bowed head grave as through a telescope
as if aware of danger; for quite soon,
perhaps, we dump our rubbish on the moon.
The new dark ages have been fiercely lit
to banish shadow and the difficult spirit;
yet here, an hour from the night-shining city
ablaze with its own close-knit electricity,
sporadic pinpoints star the archaic night
older and clearer than any glow we generate.

    Outside the exhausted kids have wandered home;
the house is quiet, calm till the next storm:
when the time comes and if the coast is clear,
work in some sort of order, let me hear
the cries of children playing but not too near.
Tick of real time, the dark realities
in the unreality of the mental gaze;
a watery murmur, a drip of diesel oil,
night silence listening to the dozy soul,
the waves' confusion in the void. 'No dice,'
said Einstein; but each bit of rock might claim
a different origin if it took its time,
the slightest life with its amoebic wobble
might tell us otherwise if it took the trouble
and even the tiniest night-rustling pebble
might solve the mystery if it had a voice;
for everything is water, the world a wave,
whole populations quietly on the move.

    Will the long voyage end here among friends
and swimming with a loved one from white strands,
the sea loud in our veins? It never ends
or ends before we know it, for everyone
'stands at the heart of life, pierced by the sun,

and suddenly it's evening' (Quasimodo);
suddenly we're throwing a longer shadow.
The hermit crab crawls to its holiday home;
dim souls wriggle in seething chaos, body
language and new thought forming there already
in hidden depths and exposed rock oases,
those secret cultures where the sky pauses,
sand flats, a whispery fringe discharging gases,
a white dish drained by the receding sea
and trailing runic whips of tangled hair
brushed and combed by the tide, exhaling air.
No, this is Galápagos and the old life-force
rides Daz and Exxon to the blinding surface.
Down there a drenching of the wilful sperm,
congenital sea fight of the shrimp and worm
with somewhere the soft impulse of a lover,
the millions swarming into pond and river
to find the right place, find it and live for ever.

John McAuliffe
Harbour Lights

'Go wandering with your stick on the back road, / you start with a ruined convent school, a tough / chough cursing you from a lichen-speckled roof' and I am again making that uphill walk past the ramparts of the old convent where my aunt taught for decades. What I love, though, is how the poem surges past the convent, its country walk taking in 'a flash of foam like Gray's *Great Wave at Sète*', 'the bird-voiced tinkle of a hidden spring' and (as the poem's metamorphic appetite grows); the material, under a little pressure, offering what Frost calls 'unexpected supply', the discovery of another life: 'a writhing Daphne hawthorn, hands and hair / mute but articulate in the Atlantic air, / chained in the ivy strings that bind her there / while somebody takes shape in the heat haze: / a young woman in tracksuit and running shoes.'

This site-specific poem drifts, sideways, suddenly, into the big picture, conjuring and collapsing time and space (hawthorn → Daphne → runner), travelling out imaginatively to different epochs and other geographies, scaling up from its particular instance of life by the sea: 'midsummer light shifting its general blaze / sets in a secret thicket of hazel trees, / on garden sheds and lined *pre-Cambrian* rock / red as the wavy roof tiles of *Languedoc*' (my italics).

In 'Harbour Lights' Mahon's established mastery of stanza is set aside for something less structured, more open: to the elements, to a lifetime's learning, to passing thoughts. And the Lowellite emphasis on the crucible of the self, of what Keats called the 'vale of soul-making', is no longer the structuring crux of the poem; the poem's 'shifts' and transformations are displaced to the natural world, its verbal pyrotechnics 'out there', always going on without us: 'strange currents circulate in these calm waters'; 'The orchard withers but the birds sing on', 'a whining saw spins free / and the wild soul flies from a stricken tree'; and always, prompted by this ceaseless activity, 'thought incubates'.

And the actions of the poem's speaker are humbler than the drenching, swarmingly populous dialectics of the natural world. Look at the verbs attached to the poem's speaker, many of them without even a subject 'I': 'Re-reading', 'watch', 'study', 'revisit', 'listen', 'toy', 'slope', 'note', 'hear' ... The poetics of 'Harbour Lights' might be compared to a passive house, existing at the mercy of local resources — but the strange thing about this 'passive house' is how highly engineered it is: long discursive sentences loosely stitched into combinations of couplet, tercet and *abab* rhymes, a mind stretching itself, and still able to hit that ecstatic, clarifying note: 'White page, dark world; wave theory; moon and pines.'

What is the word to describe this poem's (new) imaginative method? Not so much lightning-struck, although the poem is periodically lit and seized by insight. Maybe *tidal* covers its myriad perspectives: a beachcomber walking where the tide has withdrawn; a lighthouse-keeper scanning the brimming horizon; a wave-watcher, asking what's turning towards us here on the shore.

Jean Rhys at Kettner's

1

I'm crouching here in the corner, a kind of ghost
but safe with my Craven 'A' and Gordon's gin,
wearing a cloche hat and an old fox fur
and skimming *Vogue* with my distracted air.
The rush-hour crowd a hail storm ushers in
heaves at the bar like flotsam in flat seas
(I looked it up: *sargaço*, n., Portuguese)
and scares me slightly in the window seat
where I shiver, no doubt looking a bit lost
remembering cane fields in Dominican heat,
a gone-with-the-windward isle of the unblest,
the harsh plantations and the dark voyage
somewhere I lived once in another age —
with thunder, magic and the scent of jasmine.

2

Not easy being a woman in the old world —
the quick presumption, the frank stare as though
one achieved little on this earth, at least
little of what the wise world calls achieving.
Reader, I was a tedious, nightmare guest
who never learned the common art of living
but died triumphant and amazed at how
the secrecies I harboured as a child,
under the skin, were recognized at last.
'Writing I don't know; other things I know':
what children now in the gardens of Roseau?
Blown there by the discredited trade winds,
bewitched, bewildered, in at least two minds,
we found no true home in our chosen west.

3

The pianist plays show numbers and thirties jazz.
A slave in my turn, one to be bought and sold,
once hot and anxious, then aghast and cold,
I'd come here with the other chorus girls,
each in a short skirt and a string of pearls,
and men whose eyes were an anonymous glaze.
A life of boarding houses and cheap hotels
and I snag like a torn bag in a thorn-field
snapping and scratching, fighting to keep sane
in a new age; and so the soul survives.
Released at last, I lived out my two lives
between the water and the *vie en rose*:
the bottles ting-a-ling between hedgerows,
a draughty house at the end of a country lane.

Michelle O'Sulllivan
Jean Rhys at Kettner's

A trio of sonnets, the poet fathoms Rhys's comeback from the dead, yet she's framed, as the title suggests, in the famed Soho literary institution that was Kettner's. Like many a Mahon poem, there's his signature pattern of speech negotiating as it were *in media res* '. . . a kind of ghost / but safe with my Craven 'A' and Gordon's gin, / wearing a cloche hat and an old fox fur / and skimming *Vogue* with my distracted air'. An immediate ambience, we're taken so quickly that the intimate air could almost be stifling but for the movement that saves it from being static, the richness of the form, the rhyme and slant rhymes make for an almost visceral kind of reading as if we're with the crowd that the hail storm has ushered in, as if we're eyes and shoulders beside Rhys not heaving 'at the bar like flotsam in flat seas / (I looked it up: *sargaço*, n., Portuguese)'; the layering of discretional referencing, her biography and literary works, 'remembering cane fields in Dominican heat, / a gone-with-the-windward isle of the unblest, / the harsh plantations and the dark voyage / somewhere I lived once in another age / with thunder, magic and the scent of jasmine', make what might have been an unremarkable portrait; there is, after all, the economy of the situational real time and the almost quiet talk, an abiding presence.

Out of Kettner's, perhaps a more inward change of tone commences in the second sonnet. Mahon registers (or rather re-registers) Rhys's existence, 'Not easy being a woman in the old world', despite 'the quick presumption, the frank stare', it's a sideways look that turns the reflection, the perception of Rhys's voice and her work and almost as if it were an intimate aside, the 'frank stare' doubling the frank stare of what might be viewed or heard as confessional that leads to the direct address: 'Reader, I was a tedious, nightmare guest / who never learned the common art of living', the accumulation of detail from smaller details something akin to a Vanitas painting, it reads almost as a triple-fold on the work and life: at one turn it plays on Brontë's *Jane Eyre* and Rhys's much-celebrated re-working in *Wide Sargasso Sea*, and the grimmer home truth(s) of life itself: Rhys, by some accounts, was a nightmare guest given as she was to drink and bouts of depression. The tone, an almost defeated but not-quite-defeated-yet air, culminates in the confessional last line, 'we found no true home in our chosen west'. The 'we', of course, being open to multitudes. There's a reminiscent air, perhaps, of the proprietor in 'The Chinese Restaurant in Portrush' who whistles 'a little tune, dreaming of home', may be remiss and may be not, to think of that whistled tune here, but I sense something of the humanity of Mahon in these lines and generosity too, a kindness of sorts. In the end I come to find an elegance in Mahon, not so much in the sense of kid gloves, rather what might be the muter finesse of his own identification.

We return to the corner; Rhys has ceased skimming *Vogue*. The show numbers and jazz tunes have been eclipsed, and despite being at 'once hot and anxious, then aghast and cold,' suggestion over amplification builds and the sketch of biographical detail culminates in the last sonnet's turn: 'and I snag like a torn bag in a thorn-field / snapping and scratching, fighting to keep sane / in a new age'. Unlike the 'men whose eyes were an anonymous glaze', and despite the grittier details of Rhys's life and fiction, there's a specific care in the handling of the images that expresses as much about Mahon as they do about Rhys: 'and so the soul survives'. *Sans* the sordid mess of judgements, and/or base conviction, Mahon's Rhys is instead released, beautifully human and colourfully intact; despite the bottles and the draughty house I can't see the last sonnet (indeed the entirety of the poem) as anything but an optimistic sunburst. It carries all the Mahon hallmarks, where 'nothing is random, and nothing goes to waste', where the masonry's ever immaculate.

A Quiet Spot

We tire of cities in the end:
the whirr and blur of it, so long your friend,
grows repetitious and you start to choke
on signage, carbon monoxide, the hard look.
You always knew it would come down
to a dozy seaside town —

not really in the country, no,
but within reach of the countryside,
somewhere alive to season, wind and tide,
far field and wind farm. 'Wrong life,' said Adorno,
'can't be lived rightly.' The right place
is a quiet spot like this

where an expanding river spills,
still trout-rich, from the dewy hills
of Cork, still fertile in a morning mist.
So, do you pause to congratulate yourself
out here at the continental shelf,
far from the hysteria,

on the perfect work-life balancing act
you've found after so many a fugitive year
of travel? If so, let the pause be brief.
Gaia demands your love, the patient earth
your airy sneakers tread expects
humility and care.

It's time now to go back at last
beyond irony and slick depreciation,
past hedge and fencing to a clearer vision,
time to create a future from the past,
tune out the babbling radio waves
and listen to the leaves.

Peter Fallon
A Quiet Spot

Derek Mahon's more stately stanzas are so formal they wear tuxedos. Frequently they have cummerbunds and bow ties too.

'A Quiet Spot' is a pure and perfect example of his late style. Five stanzas, seven sentences, display the grace and fluency of his syntax and the clarity of his thinking as it evolves. It opens with three rhyming couplets but, as the thought grows, the *aa, bb* and *cc* relax into *d, ee, d* and *ff* and variations of such flourishes without compromising their binding effects. The rhymes are full, internal — 'whirr and blur' — and half. In one instance, *literally* half as 'mist' echoes the first syllable of the word 'hysteria'. The 'it' of line two might be 'them' but the use of the singular concentrates the subject matter.

The pronouns are magnetic. The opening 'we' — first person plural — might easily be singular. The 'you' of the second and subsequent stanzas might easily be 'I'. But the poem is speaking for more than one person.

Derek Mahon's poems move effortlessly between the natural world ('the expanding river', 'the leaves') and the world of thought and imagination. Such is their reach they embrace perennial aspects of nature (and staple tropes of lyric poetry), the utterly modern, the man-made 'wind farm' and contemporary concepts of Gaia's demands. How could he not be drawn to Adorno, the mid-century thinker (and, let's not forget, composer) renowned for his critique of what he called ' the culture industry'? He implicates his aphoristic observation without a change of beat. What other poet could fuse so seamlessly the word 'sneakers', with its nod to Yeats's 'tread (ing) softly', with the word 'Gaia' in the same sentence?

His poems move amphibiously from the lights of a harbour to 'the patient earth', indeed anadromously (that is, inhabiting salt and fresh water) from the Aegean ('The Sea in Winter' and 'Beyond the Pale'), the Irish Sea ('Beyond Howth Head', 'A Swim in Co. Wicklow') and the sea around Rathlin to rivers ('Heraclitus on Rivers', 'the expanding river . . . still trout-rich' of the poem under review), lakes ('Ovid in Tomis', 'Girls on a Bridge') and rain water ('Rain', another 'Rain', 'Rain Shadows' and the orchestral recreation of an 'angry downpour' in 'The Thunder Shower').

Ideas from 'A Quiet Spot' appear in even later poems — 'with no desire for city life / the traffic chaos, the grim crowd' ('After Swift') — and the poem's title recurs in 'Xanadu' in his last collection, far from the refuge the poet found in The Grove in Kinsale after 'so many a fugitive year / of travel' — 'a quiet spot far from the haze / of hot Dadu — Beijing as is'. But these are not repetitions — they are reminders and reinforcements of the unity of his work.

The deceptively light music of 'A Quiet Spot' finds its author in 'the right place', 'a dozy seaside town', where he achieved that 'clearer vision'. The poem begins with a description of a place, a landing place, and moves into the evocation of a state of mind. It ends in a hard-won wisdom, as cautious, consoling and satisfying as it is instructive, that is clearly and generously handed on.

A Clearing

A clearing in the wood
beyond technology, with two
car doors disintegrating in a ditch;
a listening light, domain of fox and witch
and, stiff with sudden tension, you
who dubiously intrude,

fondly imagining
like someone in a fairy story
strange beings — *sídhe, fianna*, dwarves, elves —
will part the leafy boughs to show themselves,
to shed light on the mystery
and let the magic in.

The glade, an open space
alive with immanent potential, pours
impersonal warmth into your narrow field
of sense; but something vital is withheld.
You wait, but nothing notable occurs
in this mysterious place —

or seems to occur, although
a wood-wide web is hard at work
reporting on your mischievous invasion
while secret presences obscured by sun,
revealed by shade, define the dark
and shine with their own glow.

What on earth shall we do
with this silent conventicle?
Install a picnic table, a building site?
No, this is where the angel will alight.
Just let it be, let be, until
the avatar is due.

Tom French
A Clearing

It was woodsy, but it was not 'the woods'.
— Jonathan Raban, *Bad Lands: An American Romance*

I see woods a stone's throw from the Beltany stone circle close to Raphoe and the light slanting through those trees when I look at the image of the painting by Donald Teskey which faces 'A Clearing' in *Rising Late* (2017). It was in the early days of the mobile phone and we were lost. One of our party dialled home on the other side of the country, the landline in the hall rang, connection happened and a loved voice spoke.

Not surprisingly, all that miraculous call managed to do was share the news that we were in a wood and could not find our way out. That someone else knew did not help a blind bit. Thus was the miracle of connectedness revealed. We were, if anything, even more lost *after* the phone call than before *because* someone else, who was not also lost, knew.

I would like to stand in front of that Teskey image in the flesh and get lost in it. Poem and painting place you at the edge to dwell on the phenomenon of light, on the beautiful paradox of 'secret presences obscured by sun, / revealed by shade', that 'define the dark / and shine with their own glow'. Nothing is explicit. He has left his body behind him. He is a consciousness on the verge. In the shadows of this poem is another —

> *Gaia demands your love . . .*
>
> *It's time now to go back at last . . .*
>
> *time to create a future from the past . . .*
>
> *and listen to the leaves.*
> — 'A Quiet Spot'

130

You could call it secular mysticism but it might be better not to call it anything. The words only get in the way. As with the best prayers in the literature, I don't want to understand it more than I do. I would sooner it entered me. It took me long enough to realize that the beauty and brightness of 'the far cities' depend on their being 'far'. So I hold out the same hope for this clearing.

The reader is granted a glimpse of the mind of the master at work. The definite article that preceded 'ditch' in the poem's first appearance becomes indefinite in *Against the Clock* (2018). While an indefinite article that introduced 'wood' becomes definite in the finished version. What does not change is the indefinite nature of 'a listening light', that beautiful synaesthesia. Between first appearance and final form 'A Clearing' acquires a whole second stanza to accommodate the uselessness of whatever preconceptions the human presence in the woods might harbour.

Whatever we may have thought before, now we know we can park whatever we were 'fondly imagining' and get out and walk. (The stone circle is behind me in my mind only for as long as I walk in a straight line.) If we stay long enough and keep our peace and just let be, the means by which we were transported will succumb to a kind of natural justice and wind up 'disintegrating in a ditch'. In the absence of encumbrances all that will remain then will be light and consciousness. And then just light.

It reads like a late *ars poetica*, a corrective even to Hughes' 'midnight moment's forest'. Here it is 'you' who enter the fox's domain, 'you / who dubiously intrude'. The something else that is alive is the light.

In the 1991 *Poetry Review* interview with William Scammell, Mahon, referring to himself as 'a slip of the pen', offered 'three tentative suggestions for the beginner' —

1) *Hide*
2) *Work at the happiness*
3) *Publish posthumously*

It was funny and he wasn't joking. In the end, magisterially, he achieved that hat-trick. Unlike the derelict beach hut and the abandoned wreck the edge of the clearing is not a place to hide.

He has been coming here, in one shape or form, all of his life. 'A Clearing' suggests that the secret is not to enter it, that the voice that is speaking is wary of intrusion and not lost, that it knows its way and what 'to do' when it gets there. As disclosure the poem is as beautiful as one is likely to encounter.

On the edge of the clearing, in 'this silent conventicle' afforded by Mahon's consummate artistry, 'angel' and 'miracle' arrive on the tip of his tongue and, tentatively, enter his lexicon.

And the beautiful conceit is that the edge of the clearing is still surely the woods.

Triad for Shane MacGowan

1 A RAINY NIGHT IN SOHO

A film crew have been working on a sordid
story of rape and murder in the brick lane
behind Ingestre Court, but slashing rain
has forced them to leave off and now it pours
on empty pavements and on blistered doors
unpainted since the Pogues first recorded
'A Rainy Night in Soho'. Two disorientated
drinkers, shoulders hunched against the wind,
head down uncertainly to Leicester Square
past sleeping shapes in corners of Greek St.
Tonight it's dismal even in the West End;
the squat's unheated and the cupboard bare.

2 FAIRYTALE OF NEW YORK

The drying-out clinics fill up in December;
once more it's that traumatic time of year.
The drugs are handed out in strict rotation
and the jakes locked except for diarrhoea.
She fell in love there, does she still remember,
and watched the snow on Seventh Avenue,
thrown up by buses, change to hail and rain
like bright tears on a grimy windowpane.
She soon checked out but what were we to do?
Steam drifted from underground and lights
danced in the Hudson. We were hungry then
but happy too in the dark days and nights.

3 BROUGHT UP TO AGITATE

Kirsty, 'brought up to agitate', sang along
to your now thirty-year-old punk Christmas song
for the last-minute shoppers splashing round
the supermarkets of some dirty old town.
A chap in the chipper claiming he was Elvis,
the girl in the video section, indeed all of us,
remembered her tough glamour in the eighties,
her pre-electric sound and brisk asperities,
when that Gonzalez' vicious speedboat ran
her down in the warm waters off Yucatán.
Her trenchant style is what we most recall
together with the names Seeger and MacColl.

Gerard Smyth
Triad for Shane MacGowan

Derek Mahon's diverse range of subjects, his erudition and wide field of vision, as well as his constantly refocused curiosity all point to a poet who, as Whitman wrote of himself, encompassed 'worlds and volumes of worlds'. When he declared that 'Everything aspires to the condition of rock music' (Section XI, *The Yellow Book,* now 'Decadence') it may have been with tongue-in-cheek, but I have always found particular delight in his engagement with pop and rock culture, as relevant and copious a source of poem material as the art of Pieter de Hooch or Paolo Uccello.

From decade to decade his antennae kept tabs on the ever-changing state of the zeitgeist. His alertness to the 'heavy metal that rocked the discothèques' ('Rock Music'), the 'bouzouki music of Mikis Theodorakis' ('October in Hyde Park'), or Paul Simon as 'the voice of an age' ('St Cecilia's Day') suggests a poet of endless wonder and open mind, one who made no distinction and saw no disjunction between the common and profound. When he presents us with that self-mocking version of his younger self 'snarling in my blue suede shoes' it might not be a joke.

An old pop song from the bygone era of Frank Ifield and Clodagh Rodgers may be the 'subliminal sublime', but it can also express the same existential anxiety as an image or phrase from Beckett. Björk, his 'dark swan / of snow' . . . 'dark swan of ice' belongs in a poem as much as Elizabeth Bowen or Synge, Bach or Buxtehude.

His 'Triad for Shane MacGowan' takes on two of the most iconic Pogues' songs and re-imagines them in the rich sound of his own voice. It is not merely an exercise in allusion. He truly honours the songs and their writer by creating his own variations, extending the imagery and evoking their mood in the style of his striking impressionism.

MacGowan's songs provide ideal settings for a poet of Mahon's temperament and vision to respond to; both writers capture visual detail in ways that are evocatively cinematic. 'Rainy Night in Soho' has something of the atmospherics of a Mahon poem (a whole essay could be dedicated to the rain in his poetry). They both fit in as habitués and observers of this half-lit urban world.

The drama and broody attitude of MacGowan's 'Rainy Night . . . ' and 'Fairytale . . . ' lyrics are echoed back to us in the form of Mahon's elegant formality and artfulness. Where MacGowan hears the 'wind whistling all its charms', Mahon sees 'two disorientated / drinkers, shoulders hunched against the wind'.

The third section takes us into an altogether different frame with his remarkably distilled synopsis of the short life and tragic death of MacGowan's recording sidekick, Kirsty MacColl, recalling her 'tough glamour in the eighties' and 'trenchant style', two utterly apt descriptions. These three interlinked poems — brisk in cadence, taut in structure — embody the same 'concentration and crystallization' that Mahon admired in the short poems of his New York friend, Samuel Menashe.

Ophelia

It started at nine in the morning as things do.
The eye of the cyclone remained out at sea
but we got the hard edge as it hit the coast
and, anti-clockwise, strove to devastate
a province; the lights failed and slates flew
while I sat it out here in 'excited reverie'
listening to climate change doing its work
with a stereophonic front of punitive rain.
Too much of water, fierce 'Ophelia', when
sea overwhelms our shaky earthworks. (Who
names storms, who names the winds and stars?)
No birds sing in this ominous half-dark.
We wait for daylight in the daylight hours
and, reading by candlelight as in other ages,
picture the whirling vortex, the wave surges
storming ashore; the roaring blitz of it.
It must be a sign of something, but of what?
The death of world civilization, I suppose,
and man-made climate is the evident cause —
which raises the grim question of what next?

Now lights come on and the fridge shakes,
the phone speaks in a tone of huge relief;
whatever was under wraps returns to life.
Everything picks up with the sky at rest
and nothing to scare us for a while at least.
A bit like Key West in the strange aftermath,
whipping and dripping, the storm took a path
due north and died at last over Donegal,
just a high whistling wind like any gale,
nothing remarkable. Maybe Ophelia too
was nothing special, merely first of a new
series of weather events to be lived through.
Cyclones, of course, shouldn't come up this far
into our mild, predictable temperate zone

but rage down there below the blue horizon
like fire and pestilence; yet here they are,
one further import from the Angrian shore.
    Ophelia, royal girlfriend not the wind,
withdrew to nature like a sensible maid
but chose a flowing stream and willow shade —
a dubious option, not the best of choices,
and one she'd have refused in her right mind;
but it does get harder by the year to find
sanctuary from the clamour of crazed voices.
So shut the hatches, fill the shelves and hoard
candles against the dark time coming on
when hubris reaches for the infinite spaces
in a true cyclone spun by fatal industries
with this one filed as just an autumn breeze,
one of many before the real thing began.

Thomas McCarthy
Ophelia

'The wind that blows these words to you / bangs nightly off the black-and-blue / Atlantic' wrote Derek Mahon in one of his earliest poems, 'Beyond Howth Head', published as a Poetry Ireland Editions II by the Dolmen Press in 1970. The ocean wind is always blowing in Mahon's poetry, whining under the door at Achill, the gale-force wind of Portstewart or the shore beneath the Mournes; bringing everything in its air that might threaten 'the plain Protestant fatalism of home', as he wrote in 'A Bangor Requiem'. Mahon always comes to poetry at 'the far west of human life' as he put it in his version of a Houellebecq poem 'The Clifden Road'. Wind is at its most powerful and dangerous at the edge of things, the hinterland of sea and seashore, the places where shutters are rattled and safety is challenged. Ocean wind, especially, seems more violent and desperate than any other wind; wind raids the shore of poetry at night, but then offers many poetic clearances after the break of day; opportunities of light, or, as Terence Brown once wrote in addressing Mahon's poetry: 'Light breaking through on desolate shores and bleak places.'

The storm 'Ophelia' of Derek Mahon's poem, published in *Against the Clock* (2018) was no ordinary old storm. It was an extra-tropical hurricane, the most easterly of its kind, that hit the Irish coast on October 16th, 2017, with storm winds of up to 156km/h recorded by the Cork Harbour weather-station at Roche's Point. It took human life and flooded coastal towns in the South:

> *It started at nine in the morning as things do.*
> *The eye of the cyclone remained out at sea*
> *but we got the hard edge as it hit the coast*
> *and, anti-clockwise, strove to devastate*
> *a province; the lights failed and slates flew*

while I sat it out here in 'excited reverie'
listening to climate change doing its work . . .

The poet sheltered in his tower, that Yeatsian moment, is
captured deftly and ironically. And not just Yeats, but the
very modern awareness of climate change, is included in the
poet's first view of what is happening. This fierce 'Ophelia'
of a storm makes him wonder who names storms, who
named this one so inappropriately. The poem goes on to
track the storm, 'the roaring blitz of it', and then compares
the aftermath, the scene ashore, to that of Key West after
a tropical hurricane. But then, after the storm's departure
at Donegal, the poet returns to a quieter ending, the suicide
of the other, the literary, Ophelia who 'chose a flowing
stream and willow shade'. This was a quiet ending 'she'd
have refused in her right mind'. The poem becomes a medi-
tation on the wider meaning of that name 'Ophelia'. It
yearns for answers now, like the 'royal girlfriend' who
sought sanctuary 'from the clamour of crazed voices'. The
poet wonders about the hubris of those 'fatal industries'
that drive these violent Ophelias ashore, violent endings
that may be 'one of many before the real thing began'. This
is a perfect storm, then, one of Mahon's best, combining as
it does all of those characteristic Mahon preoccupations of
shelter, of survival, of intimately human and widely circadian
rhythms.

Smoky Quartz

Thanks for the present; everything will be grand
now that I have this dark crystal at hand
to ground me with its 'strong link to the earth'.
Promising resolve and equanimity both
with its positive vibe and spiritual energy,
it works to relieve anxiety and lethargy,
helps heart and nerves, the whole constitution,
promoting tolerance and concentration.

It's a mysterious thing, transparent and opaque
like life, with faint patches of yellow light
moving around, though mostly it's black smoke
as if from buses burning at a riot,
a crippled oil rig or the world at night.

Though never used in the old crystal sets
it is its own radio and radiates
creative waves between the earth and ether,
soul and material substance. I hold it tight
in the left hand to activate the right.

Grace Wilentz
Smoky Quartz

The gift of a crystal sits on the fault line between new age 'woo woo' and sincere belief. Derek Mahon's 'Smoky Quartz' opens with a distinct note of irony: 'Thanks for the present; everything will be grand / now that I have this dark crystal at hand.' Sceptics aren't wrong of course — people assign all sorts of ludicrous powers to crystals. Indeed, a whole industry has sprung up around them. It's not hard to find a health-food-store-cum-holisitc-centre in any town in Ireland where you can pick up a packet of brown rice, some incense and a tarot deck. And as the first stanza progresses, with its neat rhyming couplets, the poem inhabits and exposes the language of the commodification and marketing of the crystal as an object. Its packaging is quoted (not without further irony) for proclaiming its 'strong link to the earth' before promising relief for a litany of parts of the body and forms of suffering, not unlike the panaceas deceptively marketed by snake oil salesmen of lore and yore.

But, in the second stanza, the poem turns. The hefty eight lines of the first break into two lighter stanzas of just five lines each. The neat rhyme scheme unravels as the poet turns his attention from the packaging to the crystal, seeing it with his own eyes. In the hand, it is strange and beautiful, both 'transparent and opaque' with 'patches of yellow light / moving around, though mostly it's black smoke'. And though these visuals conjure the magician, the poet sees in the smoke not illusion but our very real and challenged world: 'buses burning at a riot, / a crippled oil rig or the world at night'. The last image is perhaps the most arresting — when the sun sets over one continent it shines on another. At no moment is the world ever entirely 'at night', and we all hope it stays that way. This is one of many reminders throughout *Washing Up* (in which the poem first appeared) of the fragility and contingency of continued human existence on our mistreated planet.

In the final stanza the act of looking goes deeper and becomes about knowing. The poet recalls the properties of quartz that really do make it among the most useful of crystals. Indeed, quartz is present not just in 'the old crystal sets' but in our watches, pressure gauges, and in tools for the study of optics. And beyond these uses the poet recalls the shared consensus among many traditions that do believe crystals to be healing and enlivening. Here, we understand that scepticism has been left behind, and we are firmly in a place of belief. Through believing in the power of this natural object, poet transforms into magician, holding the crystal 'tight / in the left hand to activate the right', and in doing so reminds us that although much of our world has been commodified, commercialized and divvied up for sale, beyond the price tags and the branding our natural world retains ungraspable mystery and infinite value.

Another Cold Spring

Another cold spring —
the same as last year,
the previous year also,
a late storm papering
the daffodils with snow
and leaving the sky clear.

We can't depend upon
the meteorology from one
month to the next, the seasonal
graph of established weather
having been since revised
or scrapped altogether;

but when could we ever?
We know how to make do
with what the skies bestow;
hence the bluff stoicism,
routine if you prefer,
built into the system.

Another cold spring, though,
audible day and night
beneath a hanging bough,
bursts from the undergrowth,
once a monastic site
or anchoritic bower.

The water is spring-clean,
freezing to hand and mouth
straight from the dark earth,
fresh from an open field,
undoctored, undefiled,
lime-filtered, crystalline.

It has been flowing there
for ages out of mind,
this secretive, demure
whisper in the wind,
a tiny field of force
and an unfailing source

of what, the numinous?
Perhaps the 'spiritual'
if the old word retain
some of its former use,
analogous to the virtual
plainsong of a drain.

Tree-shaded from the sun
it stays icy cold when
air temperatures improve,
refusing to submit
anything of its nature
to the hot world above —

as if to say, 'This slight
outpouring isn't meant
for your enlightenment
but for my own delight;
still, if it tastes right,
take of it what you want.'

Aifric Mac Aodha
Another Cold Spring

'Another Cold Spring' appears in Derek Mahon's final collection, *Washing Up*. It follows on from the title poem and addresses the same theme — the 'bluff stoicism' he needs to bluster this world's routines.

In an earlier spring poem, 'Spring in Belfast', Mahon tells us that one part of his mind 'must learn to know its place'. That yearning informs his last collection, too, where the keynote of spring is how cold it is. Here, 'a late storm papering / the daffodils with snow' nods to Horace and the Latin poet's 'fierce winter slackening its grip'. This is a post-Horatian world, however, one where we have meteorology charts, where sacrifices to Faunus are a thing of the past, and where even the word 'spiritual' can only just about be countenanced in inverted commas. Still the modern and the ancient world continue to rub up against each other — although brilliantly, in 'virtual / plainsong', Mahon allows the monastic and the digital to reside together, but not quite side by side.

'Another Cold Spring' swerves on a pun. The season, of course, and then, that other spring, the holy well, the source that remains true and untouched by 'the hot world above'. In the fourth stanza, he tweaks his title (and first line), 'Another cold spring, *though*' (my italics). From this point on Mahon's subject matter ceases to be about the season and veers into graphless territory. Solemn adjectives such as 'undoctored, undefiled' outplay the arch tone of lines like 'The water is spring-clean, / freezing to hand and mouth':

> *It has been flowing there*
> *for ages out of mind,*
> *this secretive, demure*
> *whisper in the wind,*

a tiny field of force
and an unfailing source

of what, the numinous?
Perhaps the 'spiritual'
if the old word retain
some of its former use,
analogous to the virtual
plainsong of a drain.

In this place Derek Mahon's 'bluff stoicism' meets its match. Even through the late storms he serves and remains true to the idea of 'an unfailing source'.

Note

We have presented the poems in the order of their appearance in *Collected Poems* (1999), *New Collected Poems* (2011) and (with a few exceptions) the two subsequent collections, *Against the Clock* (2018) and *Washing Up* (2020). We have followed the texts of *The Poems (1961-2020)*, all the poems Derek Mahon wished to preserve, in their final form, published earlier this year.